This
Book
Belongs To:

_____

_____

_____

TILLER
PUBLISHING

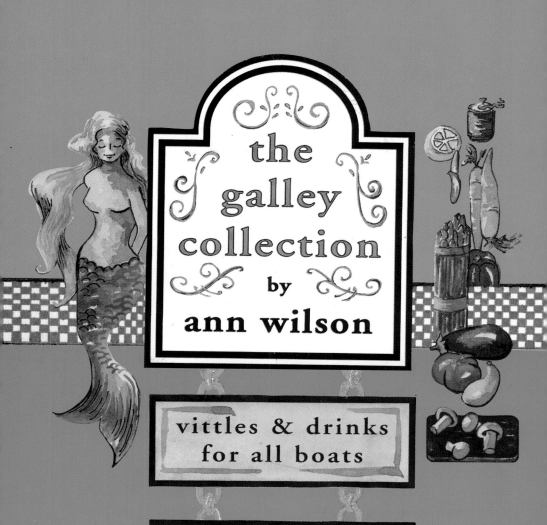

the galley collection

by

ann wilson

vittles & drinks
for all boats

illustrated by
jo gabeler brooks

Published 1998 in the United States by
Tiller Publishing, P.O. Box 447, St. Michaels, MD 21663 USA.

ISBN 1-888671-13-0

Graphic design by
Words & Pictures, Inc., 27 South River Road South, Edgewater, MD 21037

Printed in the USA by
The P. A. Hutchison Company, 400 Penn Avenue, Mayfield, PA 18433

Questions regarding the contents of this book should be addressed to:

TILLER Publishing
P.O. Box 447
St. Michaels, MD 21663
1-800-6TILLER · Fax 410-745-9743

Dedication
To my family . . .
the wind in my sails

Acknowledgements

Our gracious thanks

to Ed McBride, Jr., our counselor

to Skip Allen, *Southern Boating* magazine, for his encouragement

to many good friends, for superb support and great recipes

To Gary and Willie, The Village Market,
    for the food photo opportunity

to The Landings Yacht Club, for boating comraderie

Credits

Soup tureen . . . Grazia Dervita, Italy
Chicken Pitcher . . . Grazia Dervita, Italy, and Williams-Sonoma
Photography by Ed Coppage
      at the Delegal Creek Marina, Savannah, GA

Table of Contents

Jo Gabeler

Jo Gabeler

Jo Gabeler

Meats &
Grilled Foods - 75

Vegetables, Rice & Noodles - 103

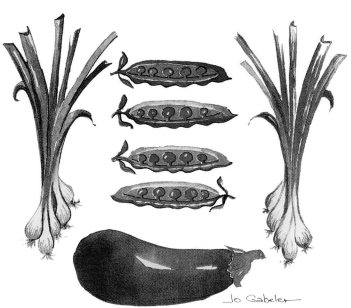

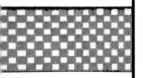

About the Author

Ann Wilson (left above) was raised in Rhode Island and lives now at The Landings on Skidaway Island, Savannah, GA. After graduating from Smith College, Ann married a career Army officer. Before dropping anchor at The Landings, the Wilsons enjoyed many moves and worldwide travel with four children. The family's love for boating also meant many boats, both sail and power. The Wilsons now cruise aboard their Grand Banks 36, *Boundless II,* carrying *Boundless, Jr.,* a 9-foot Whaler.

Combining an interest in boating with a cooking hobby, in 1989 Ann created a monthly food feature for *Southern Boating* magazine. After nearly 4 years of feature-writing, Ann decided to put favorite recipes from the articles, along with many more, in *The Galley Collection.* Previously, Ann self-published 2 cookbooks, an edited assortment of recipes for *Collectible Casseroles* and T*he Shrimp Cookbook*, co-authored with Fay Phillips in Mobile, AL. Besides thoroughly enjoying boating, Ann is seriously addicted to golf.

About the Illustrator

Jo Gabeler Brooks (right above) and Ann Wilson met at The Landings on Skidaway Island. Like Ann, Jo has four children. After graduating from Stephens College, Jo also made many moves and acquired considerable boating experience. Many of Jo's most prominent paintings are of boats and the seaside. Among her exhibits have been shows at the Watercolor Art Society, Houston, TX; Boca Raton Museum, Boca Raton, FL; and The Landings Art Association, Skidway Island, GA. Currently, Jo's paintings are displayed at the John Tucker Fine Arts Gallery in Savannah.

Jo was invited by The Elliot Museum, Hutchinson Island, Stuart, FL, and the Historical Society of Savannah to have One-Person Exhibits. In 1986 she was elected to membership in The Salamagundi Club and included in the 17th Edition of *Who's Who in American Art.* She is a signature member of The Florida Watercolor Society. The Rosenberg Library in Galveston, TX, has purchased her work, and The Moody Foundation has four of her pieces in their permanent collection. Among her awards are The Presidential Award of the Florida Watercolor Society, 1st Prize in the Galveston Art League, the Robert Simmons Merit Award in the Watercolor Art Society Houston Spring Show, and the First Hutchins-Sealy National Bank Purchase Award.

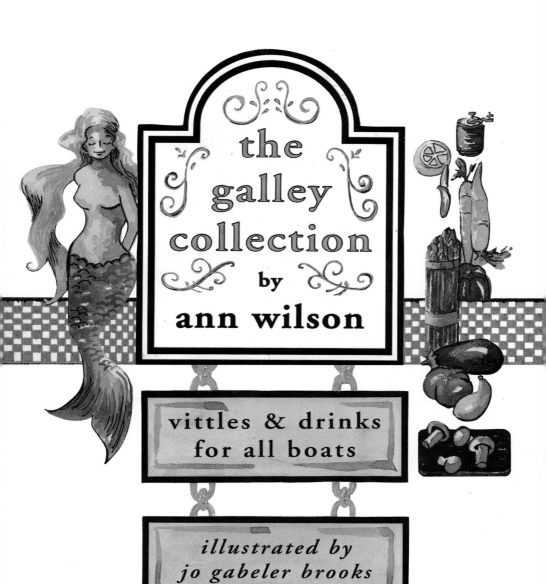

the galley collection
by
ann wilson

vittles & drinks for all boats

illustrated by
jo gabeler brooks

Introduction

*B*efore casting off, someone must decide what to take for "vittles and drinks." Ideally, the provisions will enhance the upcoming nautical experience. *The Galley Collection* has our favorite recipes, the ones we consult when it is our turn to cook.

Most productive preparation is done by boatcooks at home, creating menus, making lists, shopping for good equipment, and more. Doing some cooking ahead of time helps, too. Freezing soups and sauces, casseroles and cookies leaves the chef ready to cheer, "Anchors aweigh!"

Only a truly archaic sailor avoids commercial convenience foods. But, a reputable contemporary cook will combine convenience with a personnel touch that reflects an interest in good cooking and affection for dining companions.

Recipes for all boats? Yes. An ice chest fits into a small sailboat with gazpacho, a huge hoagie and drinks for two. Yachting friends may go all out — soup to nuts. Only the participants know who has more fun. But it is true that, in either case, a little care with the cooking enhanced the experience.

The idea here is to choose recipes that work well for you in your boat. But, keep in mind, it is not the recipe, it is the cook who controls the pot. Cooking is a creative art, with plenty of latitude for experimenting and substituting. Recipes are the guides to good meals. What better place to enjoy them than on a boat?

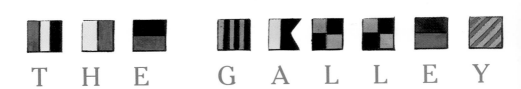

T H E   G A L L E Y

Fitting Out A Galley

cluttered, disorganized galley is miserable for a cook trying to prepare good food on a boat. Look before you leap. In a new boat, go into the galley with an open mind and a measuring tape. Measure the storage spaces, the refrigerator, the stove. Picture yourself in action. Designate a place for each thing, where it can be stored neatly and retrieved easily. Then get set up, but be flexible. Things won't be perfect right away, but the fine-tuning can be done once you swing into action.

In your present boat, if you need to, use a rainy day to reorganize. Shift things around until they are most conveniently located for the cook. And, most importantly, get rid of everything you do not use. While you're at it, replace grungy plastics, rusty utensils, stained dish towels.

Plastic baskets and bins are ideal storage containers. Select those which fit properly inside the storage compartments. They are good for separating foods, containing cleaning supplies under a sink, storing swim and snorkel gear, and many other uses.

Small, stackable food storage containers with squared off corners fit better into small cupboards and refrigerators than round ones.

Measure refrigerator space to determine the sizes of bottles needed for storing juice and milk.

Very high quality knives are worth their price. Carry a sharpening stone to keep them sharp.

Can openers do not last long. Buy a good one and carry a spare.

Dishes and glasses with rubber rings on the bottoms stay put on tippy tables.

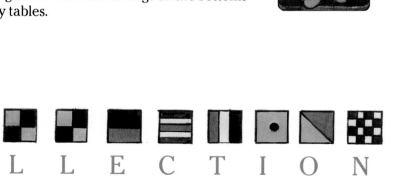

C O L L E C T I O N

Boat bags are great. Besides being useful for toting food back and forth, they catch overflow books and magazines, toys, cameras, art supplies.

Nesting baskets, buckets and bowls are useful accessories for serving snacks, apples and other food to nibble on.

Meat can be browned best in a well-heated, cast iron skillet. I always use one for pan-broiling hamburgers or steaks. It should be "seasoned" before using. Wash with sudsy water, dry. Pour about an inch of salad oil into skillet, put skillet into 275-degree oven for about an hour. Discard oil, wipe dry with paper towels. After washing an iron skillet, dry it well to prevent rusting.

A heat diffuser set on a hot burner will keep foods from burning or scorching while simmering.

For controlling kebabs on small boat grills, skewers with long handles work best. Ours are long and teflon-coated. Keep a squirt bottle of water nearby to douse flames while grilling.

A good meal is always enhanced by pleasant presentation. Tuck away some decorative items — great-looking placemats, bandannas for napkins, a red and white check vinyl tablecloth for Italian meals or pizza. Mugs are attractive for carrot and celery sticks and pickle spears. Little jugs are nice for jams. Wrap forks, knives and spoons in colorful paper napkins tied with ribbons for a snazzy boat buffet. Votive candles in colorful containers add to the glow of evening.

With an orderly galley, simple but tasty food, and a touch of style, there will be happy, congenial meals to remember.

Pots and Pans

Foil pans may be substituted for some of the following.

1 large skillet, with cover, 12-in. recommended
2 or 3 saucepans, 1, 2 and 4-qt. (1 cover)
2 or 3 nesting mixing bowls, stainless
8 x 8-in. baking pan
whistling teakettle
colander
broiler pan
1 or 2 casserole dishes, 7 x 11, 9 x 13-in.

Optional Pots and Pans

1 Silverstone-lined skillet, 8 or 10-in.
6 or 12-cup muffin pan
cookie sheet
1 or 2 9-in. round cake pans

1 large cast iron skillet
loaf pan
cooling rack
coffee pot

lobster pot
collapsible vegetable steamer
microwave cookwear

wok (I like Calphalon)
double boiler

Optional Electrical Items

Coffeepot, food processor, hand-mixer, juicer, toaster, microwave oven, blender

Flatwear

Dinner forks, dinner knives (preferably with serrated blades), teaspoons, cereal/soup spoons, salad/dessert forks, grapefruit spoons (optional), steak knives (optional).

Dishes/Glasses (unbreakable, non-skid bottoms)

Dinner plates, salad/sandwich plates, cereal/soup bowls, coffee/tea/soup mugs, 8 to 10-oz. drink glasses, wine glasses (optional), cocktail glasses or on-the-rocks glasses (optional), salad bowl, platter.

Cooking Tools (your choice)

Basting brush, beer can opener, 2 regular can openers, corkscrew, cutting board, drink strainer, long-handled fork, garlic press, grater, ice pick, 2 or 3 high-quality knives and sharpening stone, measuring cups and spoons, large mixing spoon, slotted spoon, oven thermometer, pepper mill, pot retainers for stove-top, salt and pepper shakers, salad servers, skewers, soup ladle, spatula, strainer, stove-top heat diffuser, tongs, vegetable parer, whisk.

Storage Containers

Assorted sizes, stackable, plastic, squared-off corners; beverage containers which fit the refrigerator.

Miscellaneous (your choice)

Baskets, bowls, buckets, candles, dish towels, drink holders, ice bucket, lantern, mugs and jugs, placemats, pot holders, scissors, tablecloths, trays, vase, wooden bowls.

Provisioning Tips

Provisioning for a boat trip depends upon the length of the outing or cruise, the size and type of the boat, its galley and its galley equipment. However, one thing never changes. It is best to provision using LISTS.

There is a greater need to have some menus planned and shopping lists made for boating meals than for meals at home. In the first place, you will not want a great excess of stock because it takes up too much space. But you will want the necessary ingredients to make some decent meals. So you should have with you at least the ingredients you may not find on your trip or which may be frighteningly expensive to buy.

New menus are not necessary for every trip. Once you have a variety of favorites, they can be used over and over again. And, if your shopping lists are ready, you can get away in a hurry. While everything need not be ironclad, at the very least you should have plans and provisions for days when the weather turns bad or for unexpected delays.

When cruising with friends, it is thoughtful to check with them about food preferences and dietary restrictions. Also, they may want to take part in the menu-planning and help with the cooking. That is an offer we seldom refuse. Be sure to add their requested ingredients to your shopping lists.

Stocking up on non-perishables can be done way ahead of time, if it is convenient. Some perishables may be bought a few days ahead, some must be put on board at the last minute. I make my lists from my recipe and menu selections, then refer to the following categories listed to fill out the lists.

Finally, know where you plan to put things when you bring them on board. This will help you buy the correct sizes and amounts of provisions.

Non-Perishable Categories

- **Drinks:** Bar mixes, beer, coffee, coffeemate, decaf, hot chocolate, juices, liquor, long-life milk, powdered drink mixes, soda water, soft drinks, tea, tonic, water, wines.

- **Baking:** Baking powder, baking soda, Bisquick, brown sugar, cake and cookie mixes, chocolate, cornmeal, cornstarch, extracts, flour, grits, milk (cans), nuts, pancake mix, sugar, sugar substitute.

- **Cans:** Artichokes, beans, bouillon, broths, Chinese foods, Mexican foods, fruits, ripe olives, sardines, stew, hash, oysters, soups, tomato sauce, tomato paste, tuna, vegetables.

- **Jars/Bottles:** Barbecue sauce, capers, catsup, cheeses, chili sauce, dried beef, honey, horseradish, jellies, lemon juice, Maggi seasoning, mayonnaise, mustards, olives, olive oil, Parmesan, peanut butter, picante sauce, pickles, pimentos, relish, salad oil, salad dressings, soy sauce, spaghetti sauce, syrup, Tabasco, vinegars, Worcestershire.

〜 **Cereals:** Granola, oatmeal, variety packs, etc.

〜 **Pasta/Rice:** Fettuccini, linguini, macaroni, noodles, rice, spaghetti, tortellini.

〜 **Spices/Herbs:** Basil, bay leaves, cayenne, celery seeds, chili powder, chives, cinnamon, cinnamon sticks, cumin, curry powder, dill weed, garlic salt, garlic powder, ginger, mustard, nutmeg, onion powder, oregano, paprika, parsley, pepper, peppercorns, poppy seeds, rosemary, salt, seasoned salt, sesame seeds, tarragon, thyme.

〜 **Dry Mixes, etc.:** Croutons, dip mixes, jello, noodle mixes, puddings, potato mixes, rice mixes, salad dressings, sauces, soups.

〜 **Snacks/Desserts:** Cake, candy, chips, cookies, crackers, dried fruit, Fritos, nuts, popcorn, pretzels, raisins.

〜 **Paper, etc:** Foil, foil pans, Kleenex, matches, napkins, plates/cups, plastic wrap, toilet tissue, toothpicks, towels, trash bags, zip-lock bags.

〜 **Cleaning:** 409, ammonia, bath soap, bleach, boat soap, bowl cleaner, brushes, deodorizer, dishwashing detergent, glass cleaner, laundry soap, polishes, scouring pads, scouring powder, sponges.

〜 **Health:** Antacid, aspirin, Bacitracin, band aids, Dramamine, Immodium, Solarcaine, etc.

〜 **Miscellaneous:** Batteries, candles, charcoal, charcoal lighter, citronella, clothes pins, film, games, insect repellent, lip balm, pens/paper, playing cards, scissors, sewing kit, suntan lotion.

Perishables

〜 **Produce:** Apples, bananas, grapefruit, lemons, limes, oranges, etc. Cabbage, celery, garlic, lettuce, onions, potatoes, tomatoes, etc.

〜 **Breads:** Biscuits, English muffins, French/ Italian bread, assorted. sandwich breads, pita bread, assorted rolls, tortillas.

〜 **Refrigerator/Dairy:** Butter, cream, cheeses, cottage cheese, dips, eggs, frozen foods, half-and-half, ice, margarine, milk, sour cream, whipped cream, yogurt.

〜 **Meats/Seafood:** Bacon, beef (steak, etc.), crabmeat, chicken, fish, ham, hamburger, hot dogs, lamb, lunch meats, pork, sausages, scallops, shrimp, oysters, turkey, veal.

Helpful Hints

〜 When stir-frying and pan-broiling, keep the oil and the pan hot. If too much food is added at one time, the pan and oil will cool down. The food will steam instead of searing. Keep the food moving over high heat, setting small batches aside as they are cooked. Add oil in small amounts as needed.

〜 Stir-frying is a good technique which should not be limited to Oriental cooking alone. Stir-fry a medley of fresh vegetables. Or, stir-fry strips of ham with julienne-sliced vegetables, moisten with cream, season as you wish, serve over pasta. Fajitas are basically a stir-fry. Healthful and economical, stir-frying is practical for boatcooks.

〜 It is best to use commercial, unsalted butter, or "clarified" butter which you make yourself, if the butter will be added to a very hot skillet to brown meats, poultry or seafood. Salted butter may burn too quickly. For **clarified butter,** cut butter into small pieces. Melt in a saucepan over moderate heat. Let stand a few minutes until salty solids settle to the bottom of the saucepan. Skim salty froth off the top, pour off the clear liquid, reserve the solid residue for seasoning vegetables. Refrigerate. Or beat the burning butter problem by adding a little oil to a browning skillet, then add butter. Brown in oil and butter mixed.

〜 To **deglaze** a browning skillet, after browning meat, poultry or seafood, pour off excess fat. Add a little water, broth, wine or vegetable cooking water to pan, with a few pinches of herbs, if desired, chives, parsley or garlic. Scrape up browning particles, boil liquid to evaporate until only a few tablespoons remain. The concentrate will add good flavor to a finishing sauce or broth used for braising.

〜 Freeze meats, poultry and seafood in small flat packages which stack in small boat freezers or refrigerators. I like to freeze boneless chicken breasts, chops, hamburgers, individually wrapped steaks, strips of meat ready for stir-fries, etc. The smaller the packages, the better they fit.

If poultry is thawed in the refrigerator, cook it within 2 days. Cook ground beef within 2 days, larger pieces of beef within 4 days. Do not put cooked meat or poultry back on the same plate that held raw meat or chicken.

After using it to cut raw meat or uncooked poultry, wash a cutting board with soapy water.

Tender cuts of meat which cook much faster than less tender cuts are sometimes best to buy for boat cooking, especially when the weather is hot.

Freeze stews, chili, tomato sauce, etc. in rinsed milk cartons. They keep an ice chest cool for a while and are welcome when they thaw.

Fish and shellfish must be handled extremely carefully. Cook as soon as possible after catching or purchasing. Be certain the fishing area is unpolluted and safe for fishing. Avoid cooking reef-feeding fish which may cause ciguatera. Know your supplier when it comes to seafood. And, be cautious in unfamiliar restaurants. When in doubt, avoid seafood.

A general rule for cooking fish is to allow 10 minutes per inch of thickness, 20 minutes per inch if frozen. (If baking, this will be in a preheated 350 to 375-degree oven.) Measure fish at its thickest point. If the fish is covered with a sauce, allow 5 minutes longer per inch.

Fresh crabmeat freezes well when covered with whole milk. Defrost in refrigerator, drain in colander, rinse lightly, press out moisture.

For easy storage and quick retrieval, cut iceberg lettuce into quarters and wrap in foil.

To keep produce from consuming too much storage space, remove the excess — tops from carrots, stems from parsley, outer leaves from lettuce and cabbage. Split up bunches of celery and carrots, wrap in foil or plastic wrap, or put into plastic bags. Break up bunches of broccoli and heads of cauliflower, discarding the leaves. Cut melons in half, cover with plastic wrap. Meal-making will become easier.

If leafy salad greens are washed before refrigerating, dry well, store in plastic bags with a paper towel or two to absorb excess moisture.

Cabbage keeps well. A combination of shredded white and red cabbage makes a pretty salad. Finely shredded or grated cabbage may be used in place of lettuce on sandwiches.

Fresh chopped parsley looks very nice on many finished dishes and enhances the flavor of soups, sauces and salad dressings. It will remain crisp and fresh for many days if washed, drained, blotted dry and refrigerated in a covered jar or stored in a plastic bag with a paper towel.

For dippers and salads, put washed and cut cauliflower, carrots, broccoli and radishes in zip-lock plastic bags. Cover with water, refrigerate, drain when ready to use.

Immerse tomatoes in boiling water for 15 seconds to make them easy to peel.

To delay discoloration, sprinkle surfaces of cut avocados with lemon or lime juice.

Before slicing a lemon, roll around on a table top to loosen the juice.

Spices and herbs are extremely important for making meals on a boat interesting. Store them away from sunlight, and replace when old and flavorless. Fresh herbs are wonderful. Use them when they are available.

Store the spice bottles you use all the time within easy reach. The rest may need to be tucked away. Since my spice bottles reside in a topless shoe box in a cupboard near the floor, I look down on them when I am looking for them. So, I put a little white label on the top of each bottle identifying the spice, and I keep them more or less in alphabetical order.

When doubling a recipe, taste the food before doubling the amount of salt and seasonings. Salt should be used very sparingly in any recipe calling for bouillon.

A favorite seasoning mixture is convenient to have aboard. I especially like Maggi Seasoning in a little brown bottle. Discover some new favorites of your own.

For a short trip, or an excursion calling for just a meal or two aboard, often it is best to measure out spices at home and put them into small zip-lock bags.

I often bag up all the ingredients, including a little bag of spices, for a whole meal. This is especially handy when the meal will be made primarily with canned goods. Everything is together when I need it.

To make fresh bread crumbs, tear bread into small pieces, crumble with your palms and fingertips. Dried herbs may be added to the crumbs.

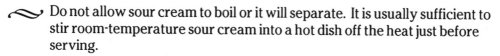

~ Do not allow sour cream to boil or it will separate. It is usually sufficient to stir room-temperature sour cream into a hot dish off the heat just before serving.

~ Plain yogurt may used in place of sour cream. Or, it may be mixed with sour cream.

~ An 8-ounce container of fruit-flavored, low-fat yogurt mixed with 1 cup cut up fresh fruit is filling and nutritious.

~ Chill cream, bowl and beaters to whip cream easily. If adding vanilla and sugar, add toward the end of beating time, after the cream has formed soft peaks. Be careful not to overbeat cream or it may separate.

Four Ways to Reduce a Sauce or Gravy:

REDUCE. Boil liquid to evaporate excess. Flavor will become more concentrated.

BEURRE MAINIÉ. In French, this is "handled butter." Mix equal amounts of flour and butter to a paste. (I use a little more flour than butter for nutritional reasons.) Drop by bits into boiling liquid, stirring until sauce or gravy is consistency desired.

FLOUR AND LIQUID MIXTURE. Spoon some hot liquid from the pan into a cup with a little flour. Stir until smooth. Slowly pour back into liquid in the pan, stirring constantly. Boil gently and continue stirring as liquid thickens. Repeat if necessary.

CORNSTARCH. It takes half as much cornstarch as flour to thicken the same amount of liquid. Mix cornstarch with water or other liquid until a milk-like consistency before adding to simmering liquid.

The Microwave Oven

*F*or convenience, a cooler galley, defrosting, reheating, and other uses, the microwave oven is a popular addition on boats today. My personal preference is to use our microwave oven for cooking vegetables, which leaves stove burners free for preparing the main dish.

Microwave cooking times vary considerably according to wattage of the oven, size and volume of containers and other factors. By storing aboard a

favorite microwave cookbook, answers to questions will be at your fingertips. I use *Micro Ways* by Jean Anderson and Elaine Hanna. It is interesting, informative and complete.

A few reminders, regardless of wattage:

∽ Stir liquids before heating so they will not erupt. Heat milk in a container larger than normal as it boils higher than normal. Microwave sauces made with cream at medium-high and stir often.

∽ When adapting recipes, reduce fat and oil by about half, liquids by a fourth. Reduce amounts of dried herbs, which intensify in flavor. May increase amounts of fresh herbs.

∽ When estimating cooking times, slightly undercook food. Allow for recommended standing time, when food continues cooking.

∽ Stir cut-up vegetables when half done. Food in center of any dish cooks more slowly than the food on outside.

∽ As a general rule, allow 2 minutes on high for 1 cup solid food in a 650-700 watt oven.

∽ Freeze foods in microwave-safe containers. Remove lids, cover with plastic wrap. Pierce wrap or turn back corner. (I think of Stouffer's container sizes and cooking times when I am guessing about the length of time to cook a dish.)

∽ To clean a microwave oven, avoid scouring pads, strong detergents and ammonia. Use warm water and a mild detergent.

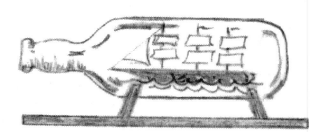

Appetizers
&
Beverages

Notes / Extra Recipes

Appetizers

Mock Boursin

    8-oz. pkg. cream cheese, softened
    1 stick butter, softened
    ¼ tsp. garlic powder
    ⅛ tsp. each: basil, marjoram, dillweed, oregano, thyme, pepper, onion salt

    Blend well with an electric beater or with a spoon. Serve with crackers or spread on French bread. *Mary Clapp.*

Cream Cheese with Cracked Pepper

    8-oz. pkg. cream cheese, softened
    4 Tbsps. butter, softened
    2 cloves garlic, minced or pressed
    ½ tsp. dried chives
    ¼ tsp. dried thyme
    About 1 Tbsp. milk if needed to thin
    Cracked pepper (coarse-ground)

    Mix all except pepper. Shape into ball, cover with pepper. Or, put mixture into a small bowl, sprinkle with cracked pepper. Bring to room temperature for easy spreading.

Liverwurst Paté

    8 oz. roll braunschweiger, softened
    8 ozs. cream cheese, softened
    1 to 2 tsps. lemon juice
    Worcestershire sauce to taste
    Grated onion (optional)

    Mix all thoroughly. If the braunschweiger has no onion mixed in, then you may add some. May use low-fat cream cheese and low-fat braunschweiger. May freeze small amounts in small dishes for impromptu cocktail hours. *Ginny Dawson.*

Cream Cheese Spreads

    Liberally cover a 3-oz. block or an 8-oz. block of cream cheese with picante sauce or hot pepper jelly or Major Grey's chutney, chopped. Serve with crackers. Or, blend 8 ozs. softened cream cheese with ½ c. picante sauce. Serve with tostitos.

Cream Cheese and Artichoke Spread

8-oz. pkg. cream cheese, softened
1½ Tbsps. cream-style horseradish
1 tsp. dried chives
Pinch cayenne pepper
14-oz. can artichoke hearts, drained

Chop 3 artichoke hearts into tiny pieces. (Use remaining artichokes in a salad.) Fold artichoke bits into cheese mixture made with remaining ingredients.

Crabmeat Spread

8-oz. pkg. cream cheese, softened
½ lb. fresh crabmeat, all shell removed
Garlic powder to taste
½ c. chili sauce
2 Tbsps. each: lemon juice and horseradish, or to taste

Gently mix cream cheese and garlic powder with crabmeat. Shape into a rounded mound on serving plate. Mix remaining ingredients for sauce.
Spoon over crab. Spread on crackers. *G. Hilmes.*

Pinwheels

Cut a thin slice of ham the length of a dill pickle, such as Heinz Original Dills. The ham should not be too thinly sliced, or it will tear. Spread ham with soft cream cheese. Wrap ham slice around pickle, about 2 complete turns. Cut into 1-inch wide pinwheels. Chill.

Spread fairly thin slices of ham or smoked turkey breast with soft cream cheese. Sprinkle with finely chopped scallions. Roll. Refrigerate. When cold, cut into 1-inch wide pinwheels.

Guacamole

2 avocados (bumpy-skinned preferred), peeled, diced
1 tsp. fresh lime juice
1 small tomato, diced
2 green onions, finely chopped
1 fresh jalapeno pepper, finely chopped
1 clove garlic, minced
Salt to taste
Additional lime juice if desired

Gently mix lime juice with avocado cubes. Fold in tomato, green onions, jalapeno pepper and garlic. Add salt, lime juice and more garlic if desired. Refrigerate covered until serving. Good with tortilla chips. *S. Gaede, adapted.*

Avocado Dip with Sour Cream

1 c. sour cream
½ c. fresh minced parsley
¼ c. finely chopped green onions
½ tsp. seasoned salt
⅛ tsp. pepper
1 large ripe avocado, mashed
½ c. mayonnaise

Mix sour cream, parsley, green onions and seasonings. Fold in the mashed avocado. If not serving immediately, push avocado seed into center of dip to prevent browning. Coat mixture with mayonnaise. At serving time, remove seed, fold in mayonnaise.

Cucumber Dip

8-oz. pkg. cream cheese, softened
1 c. mayonnaise (Hellman's preferred)
1 Tbsp. lemon juice
1 medium cucumber, peeled, diced
¼ c. chopped green onions
Dash Tabasco sauce

Mix well. Serve with vegetables, chips or crackers.

Dill Dip

    1 c. sour cream
    ¾ to 1 c. mayonnaise
    2 Tbsps. onion flakes, crushed
    2 Tbsps. parsley flakes, crushed
    1 tsp. dillweed
    1 tsp. Beau Monde seasoning (Spice Islands)

For 1¾ c. for raw vegetables or chips.

Clam Dip

    8-oz. pkg. cream cheese, softened
    6½-oz. can minced clams, drained, liquid reserved
    2 Tbsps. reserved clam juice
    1 Tbsp. fresh lemon juice
    1½ tsps. Worcestershire sauce
    2 or 3 dashes Tabasco sauce
    ¼ tsp. salt

Mix all except clams until very smooth. Mix in the clams. Good with chips or crackers.

Layered Mexican Dip

    15-oz. can refried beans
    1 c. sour cream
    1 avocado, peeled, diced
    1 c. (approximately) salsa or picante sauce
    Very finely shredded lettuce
    1 small tomato, diced
    1 c. grated Cheddar cheese
    Chopped scallions and/or ripe olives (optional)

Make thin layers of ingredients in order listed in a glass pie plate or on a large shallow plate. Serve with wide corn chips.

Dip for Shrimp

Mix ½ c. mayonnaise and ½ c. sour cream. Season with ½ tsp. each dillweed and garlic powder.

Spinach Dip

 1 c. mayonnaise
 1½ c. sour cream
 1 pkg. Knorr's vegetable soup mix, crushed
 10-oz. pkg. frozen chopped spinach, thawed, well-drained
 8-oz. can water chestnuts, drained, coarsely chopped
 ½ c. each: chopped fresh parsley, chopped green onions, finely chopped

 Mix well. Refrigerate covered several hours before serving.

Ranch Dip

 Combine 1 pkg. Original Hidden Valley Ranch Salad Dressing Mix with 1 c. each mayonnaise and sour cream. Extremely popular.

Curry Dip

 Combine 1 c. Hellman's mayonnaise with 1 tsp. curry powder, 2 tsps. lemon juice and 1 Tbsp. grated onion. Try with baby asparagus or celery sticks.

Onion Dip

 Soften 3-oz. pkg. cream cheese. Mix with cottage cheese until of good dip consistency. Add pinches of crumbled dehydrated onion soup mix until it tastes good. Refrigerate covered. *Fay Phillips.*

Horseradish Dip

 Zip up mayonnaise, a little paprika and some drained horseradish. Serve with crispy vegetable dippers.

Marinated Mushrooms

1 lb. small or medium fresh mushroom caps
⅔ c. salad oil
⅓ c. white wine vinegar
1 Tbsp. lemon juice
1 Tbsp. dried parsley
½ tsp. sugar
¼ tsp. salt
⅛ tsp. pepper
1 clove garlic, remove before serving

Make dressing for marinade. Marinate mushrooms at least a few hours, refrigerated. Drain to serve with cocktail picks. Leftovers good in salads.

Hot Artichoke Dip

14½-oz. can water-packed artichoke hearts, drained, chopped
¾ c. each: grated Parmesan, mayonnaise

Preheat oven to 350 degrees. Mix ingredients, bake in small oven-proof serving dish about 20 minutes. Good with chips, Fritos or crackers. Serves 4.

Hot Mexican Dip

8 ozs. cream cheese, softened
15-oz. can Hormel chili without beans
8 ozs. grated Monterey Jack cheese

Layer as listed in a pie plate. Bake at 350 degrees until hot, about 20 minutes. Serve with Fritos.

Hot Crab Dip or Cracker Spread

8-oz. block cream cheese, softened
1 Tbsp. milk
½ lb. fresh crabmeat, shell removed
2 Tbsps. finely chopped green onions
1 tsp. cream-style horseradish
¼ tsp. salt, pepper to taste
⅓ c. slivered toasted almonds

Combine ingredients except almonds. Spoon into shallow one-quart oven-proof serving dish, sprinkle with almonds. Bake about 15 minutes in preheated 375-degree oven. Serve with crackers.

Broiled Mushrooms

Fill bite-size mushroom caps with herbed cheese, such as Boursin, Alouette, Rondole. Arrange on foil-covered baking pan in center of oven. Broil briefly until bubbly-hot. Let cool a bit before serving. They are VERY hot.

Hot Chipped Beef Spread

2¼-oz. jar chipped beef, coarsely chopped
8 oz. pkg. cream cheese, softened
½ c. sour cream
4 green onions, chopped
¼ c. chopped green pepper
½ tsp. garlic powder (not salt)
Dash Worcestershire sauce
½ c. chopped pecans

Mix all except nuts. Spread in a small baking dish. Sprinkle with pecans. Bake at 350 degrees about 15 minutes. Spread on plain crackers.

Bacon and Water Chestnuts

5-oz. can water chestnuts, drained
¼ c. soy sauce
2 Tbsps. brown sugar
Dash powdered ginger
Bacon

Slice water chestnuts into halves if large. Soak in soy mixture about 30 minutes. Fry bacon until half cooked. Wrap water chestnuts in half strips of bacon. Secure with cocktail picks. Bake on ridged disposable foil pans or on a broiling pan in preheated 375-degree oven about 10 minutes or until bacon is cooked. These are scorching hot, cool a bit before eating. Delicious.

Brie with Almonds

Slice a thin layer from the top of a round of brie or camembert. Tuck in a layer of untoasted slivered almonds. Dot with little bits of butter. Place in oven-proof serving dish. Broil in mid-oven a few minutes to soften cheese. Serve with plain crackers.

Hot Cheese Dip

1 c. mayonnaise
1 c. grated cheddar cheese
1 small onion, finely chopped

Mix in an oven-proof serving dish. Bake at 375 until bubbly, about 15 minutes. Serve with wide Fritos or other dippers. *Ginny Kiefer.*

Marinated Brussels Sprouts

2 pkgs. frozen small brussels sprouts, cooked
2 small onions, thinly sliced
½ c. salad oil
½ c. tarragon vinegar
1 Tbsp. sugar
1 tsp. garlic salt
Additional salt if needed

Mix oil, vinegar, sugar and garlic salt. Add brussels sprouts and onions. Marinate at least overnight. Add additional salt if desired. Will keep about one week covered and refrigerated. *P. Downey*

Dolly's Crab Mold

1 can condensed cream of mushroom soup
1 pkg. plain gelatin
8 ozs. cream cheese, cubed
½ c. finely chopped celery
¼ c. finely chopped onion
1 c. mayonnaise
1 Tbsp. lemon juice
½ lb. fresh lump crabmeat,
    all shell removed

Stirring frequently, slowly heat soup with gelatin and cream cheese over low heat. Cool slightly. Mix in remaining ingredients except crabmeat. Gently fold in crabmeat. Pour into oiled 8-cup mold. Chill until firm. Bring to room temperature 30 minutes before unmolding. Dust with paprika. Serve with crackers. Easy and very festive.

Party Nibbles

6-oz. pkg seasoned croutons
6-oz. pkg. fish-shaped crackers
6-oz. pkg. pretzel twists (or smallest pretzels)
12-oz. can mixed nuts
¾ c. butter, melted
1 tsp. hickory salt or seasoned salt
¼ tsp. garlic powder

Combine croutons, crackers, pretzels and nuts in a large roasting pan (or broiler pan). Stir well. Mix melted butter, salt, and garlic powder. Drizzle over nut mixture. Stir well. Bake at 250 degrees 1 hour stirring every 15 minutes. Addictive. I keep small packages in the freezer and take to the boat. *Joan Klug.*

Beverages

M any packaged drink mixes are good and certainly useful while boating. In addition, you'll want to have on board recipes for your own favorite drinks and a small bartender's guide for unusual requests. We use a standard 1½-ounce jigger for our drinks.

The Captain's Rum Punch

3 ozs. dark rum
6-oz. can pineapple juice
6-oz. can grapefruit juice

Mix to serve 2 over ice in highball glasses.

Lynn Hartley's Painkiller

1 jigger coconut milk (Coco Lopez)
2 jiggers orange juice
3 jiggers pineapple juice
Rum to taste (Mount Gay or equivalent)
Nutmeg, freshly-grated preferred

Pour cream of coconut, juices and rum into a blender. Buzz until frothy. Pour over ice, sprinkle with nutmeg. For 2 tall drinks. Make a triple batch to serve 4.

My Favorite Bloody Mary

6-oz. can tomato juice
1 jigger vodka
2 tsps. lemon juice
½ tsp. horseradish
Generous dash each: Worcestershire, Tabasco
Celery stick for stirring

Mix and pour over ice for 1 drink. (We also like Bloody Marys made from Snappy Tom and vodka, with celery sticks for stirring and a wedge of lemon in the drinks.)

Madras

In a tumbler over ice, pour 1 jigger vodka. Fill glass with equal amounts of orange juice and cranberry juice.

Rum Breeze

Put several cubes of ice into a tall glass. Pour in a jigger of rum, then equal parts orange juice and cranberry juice cocktail. Garnish with a slice of orange, lemon or lime.

Sea Breeze

Pour 1 jigger of vodka over ice in a tall glass. Then fill with equal amounts of cranberry juice cocktail and grapefruit juice.

Mimosa

Half fill a large wine glass or champagne glass with chilled fresh orange juice, then fill glass with champagne. Finish with a splash of triple sec. Great brunch drink.

Matador

Pour 1 jigger tequila, 2 jiggers pineapple juice and 1 jigger lime juice over ice in an old-fashion glass.

Planter's Punch

Pour over ice in a glass, 1 jigger Bacardi gold rum, 2 ozs. each orange juice and pineapple juice and a dash each of Angostura bitters and grenadine. Garnish with a cherry and an orange slice.

Sangria

1 qt. red wine (Gallo Burgundy is good)
¼ c. sugar or to taste
1 sliced lemon or lime (or half of each)
2 seedless oranges, unpeeled, sliced
Club soda

Pour wine into a large pitcher. Add sugar,
stir to dissolve. Add fruit. Put about 4 ice
cubes into each tumbler or large wine glass. Add a few slices of fruit. Fill half to
three-fourths full with wine, top off with sparkling water. Serves 4.

Russian Tea

1 c. plain instant tea
2 c. dry Tang
1½ c. sugar
1 small pkg. lemonade mix (Wyler's, Kool Aid)
1½ tsps. cinnamon
¾ tsp. ground cloves

Mix well and store in an air tight container. Stir mixture well before using
2 to 3 tsps. per mug. Fill with boiling water.

Banana Sunrise

2 ripe bananas
1 c. (or 6-oz. can) unsweetened pineapple juice
or 1 c. orange juice (fresh preferred)

Blend or whisk cut-up bananas with juice. Add any other fresh fruits
desired. Great energizer. Serves 1.

Fruit Punch

1½ c. sugar
1 qt. very strong hot tea
1 qt. orange juice
1 c. lemon juice
1 liter ginger ale

Dissolve the sugar in the hot tea. Mix with the juices. Pour over a small
block of ice. Add ginger ale just before serving. *Ellen Lew*.

Swiss Mocha

    1 c. Coffeemate (powdered cream)
    ¾ c. Nestle's Qwik
    ½ c. each: instant coffee, sugar
    ¼ tsp. cinnamon
    ½ tsp. nutmeg

Mix well. Store in covered jar. Use about 1 heaping Tbsp. per mug.

Rummy Shake

    ½ banana
    2 ozs. cream
    1½ ozs. pineapple juice
    1½ ozs. light rum
    Dash grenadine

Blend thoroughly. Garnish with a cherry.

Irish Coffee

    6 ozs. strong hot coffee
    1 to 2 tsps. sugar
    1 jigger (1½ ozs.) Irish Whiskey
    Whipped cream

Add sugar to hot coffee. Stir well. Add whiskey. Top with a generous dollop of whipped cream. (REAL whipped cream in an aerosol can is very adequate.)

Viennese Coffee

    3 c. strong black coffee
    ½ c. heavy cream
    1 Tbsp. powdered sugar
    ½ tsp. vanilla extract
    4 cinnamon sticks

Whip cream until nearly stiff. Add sugar and vanilla. Continue beating until stiff. Spoon over 4 cups of coffee. Cinnamon sticks are stirrers.

Hot Mulled Wine

    2 c. cranberry juice cocktail
    1 c. water
    ½ c. sugar
    1 2-inch length of cinnamon stick
    6 whole cloves
    1 bottle red wine
    2 Tbsps. fresh lemon juice

Mix cranberry juice, water, sugar, cinnamon and cloves in a large pot. Cook over low heat, stirring occasionally, until sugar is dissolved. Simmer uncovered about 15 minutes. Remove cloves and cinnamon stick, add wine and lemon juice. Simmer until hot. About 6 cups. Great for boat parades. Keep hot in non-aluminum pot or electric coffeepot or a big thermos.

Hot Buttered Rum

    1 jigger rum
    1 to 2 tsps. sugar or to taste
    4 whole cloves
    Pinch of nutmeg (optional)
    Pat of butter
    Cinnamon stick

Put rum, sugar and cloves into a mug. Fill mug with boiling water. Sprinkle on nutmeg if desired, pop on a bit of butter, stir with the cinnamon stick.

Hot Toddy

    Lump or spoonful sugar
    Boiling water
    2 ozs. whiskey
    1 slice of lemon
    Grated nutmeg

Put the sugar into a mug. Add boiling water to about 2/3 full. Add whisky. Drop in lemon slice. Stir. Sprinkle with nutmeg.

Eggs and Poultry

Notes / Extra Recipes

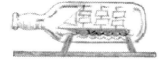

Eggs

Country Omelet

2 Tbsps. butter
1 large potato, peeled, thinly sliced, slices halved
1 medium onion, very thinly sliced
1 (additional) Tbsp. butter
3 or 4 eggs, fork-beaten with salt and pepper

Heat butter in large skillet. Sauté potato and onion slices until golden brown and cooked through, 5 to 10 minutes. Set aside, cover with foil to keep warm. Reheat skillet, add extra butter, when hot, pour in eggs. Allow eggs to set along edges, then draw edges toward center allowing uncooked mixture to spread and cook. Cook just until set but still creamy. Spoon potato-onion mixture over eggs, fold in half. Serves 2..

Creamy Scramblers with Garlic and Herbs

8 eggs
¼ c. cream or milk, salt and pepper
2 Tbsps. butter
¼ c. softened garlic-and-herb cheese (Alouette, Boursin)
¼ c. fresh chopped parsley or 2 tsps. dried
Toasted English muffins or toast

Whip together eggs, cream or milk, salt and pepper. Melt butter in large skillet, cook eggs over low heat until half done. Add cheese and parsley, stir gently until cheese melts and eggs are still soft and creamy. Spoon over toasted English muffins or toast. Serves 4 to 6.

Crab Omelet

Saute 2 Tbsps. chopped green onion and 1 Tbsp. chopped fresh parsley in 1 Tbsp. butter a few minutes. Add ½ c. lump crabmeat, keeping it chunky. Season with salt and pepper and 1 tsp. lemon juice. Use as a filling for 1 omelet made from 2 or 3 eggs. Spoon warm filling over half the omelet when eggs are set, just before folding. *George Phillips, adapted.*

Layered Omelet

No flipping or folding, just a mountain of goodness that makes a meal. Though not essential, a heat diffuser over stove burner is useful for preventing eggs from sticking or burning during the slow cooking.

4 slices bacon
3 Tbsps. butter
1 large onion, very thinly sliced
1 large ripe tomato, sliced
¼ c. chopped fresh parsley
Salt and freshly-ground black pepper
4 eggs, fork-beaten until frothy
2 Tbsps. milk or cream (optional)

Fry bacon in large skillet, drain, crumble coarsely, set aside. Melt butter in skillet, add onion rings, sauté until slightly softened. Arrange tomato slices over onions, sprinkle with parsley, season with salt and, generously, with pepper, top with crumbled bacon. Do not stir. Beat eggs with milk or cream, if desired. Pour over skillet mixture. Cook covered over lowest heat until eggs are just set, approximately 20 minutes. Serves 3 or 4. May add some grated cheddar over eggs towards end of cooking time.

Omelet with Tomato and Feta Cheese

2 eggs, 1 tsp. water, salt and pepper
1 Tbsp. butter
¼ c. crumbled feta cheese, or more to taste
1 small tomato, diced

Beat eggs with water, salt and pepper. Heat butter in small skillet, pour in eggs. Draw eggs toward center with tines of a fork, letting uncooked portion run to outside. While still creamy, add cheese and tomato. Cook briefly, fold omelet in half. Serves 1. *Jean Sexton.*

Omelet with Spinach and Mushrooms

Sauté fresh sliced mushrooms in a bit of butter. Set aside. Now, sauté fresh spinach, cut into strips or torn into small pieces, in a little butter. Set aside with mushrooms. Add eggs to bubbling butter in an omelet pan or skillet. When nearly set, cover half the eggs with mushrooms and spinach. Season with salt and pepper. Fold when eggs are set. *Jo Gabeler Brooks.*

The Nestegg

Cut a circle from the center of a slice of bread with a tumbler or paring knife. Heat 1 Tbsp. butter in medium skillet. Brown bread on one side, turn over. Break egg into cut out hole, season with salt and pepper, cook covered on low heat until egg sets. For 1.

Quiche with Ham and Cheese

2 eggs
½ c. mayonnaise
2 Tbsps. flour
½ c. milk
1⅔ c. diced ham
1 c. shredded Swiss cheese
½ c. sliced green onions
1 9-inch unbaked pie shell

Whisk eggs in medium bowl. Whisk in mayonnaise, flour and milk. Stir in ham, cheese and green onions. Pour into pie shell. Bake in preheated 350-degree oven 40 to 45 minutes. Serve hot, warm or at room temperature. *Susan Sperry-Roark.*

Deviled Eggs

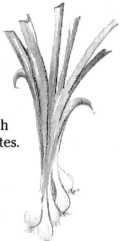

6 hard-boiled eggs
¼ c. mayonnaise
1 tsp. each: vinegar, prepared mustard
Dash pepper, paprika

Cut eggs in half, mash yolks with mayonnaise, vinegar and mustard. Season with pepper. Spoon mixture into cavities in egg whites. Dust tops with paprika. Chill, covered.

Poultry

A 3 to 3½ lb. cooked chicken will yield enough cut up chicken to serve 4. Allow 2½ to 3 lbs. assorted parts for 4. For a casserole for 4, it is enough to cook 3 large half breasts with ribs, or 1½ lbs. boneless half breasts. Cooked, cubed turkey may be substituted in most cases for chicken in casserole creations.

We stash away several 14½-oz. cans of ready-to-serve chicken broth for making sauces and soups. Also, condensed cream of chicken, celery and mushroom soups are handy. So is bouillon, either cubes or granules.

On the boat, I find it easier to poach chicken parts than to cook whole cut-up chickens. When cooking dark meat along with the white, allow the dark meat to cook an extra 5 to 10 minutes. Poached or simmered chicken parts are very handy for casseroles, salads and sandwiches.

Oven-Poached Chicken Breasts

Preheat oven to 375 degrees. Lay boneless chicken breast halves in a single layer in a baking dish. Season with salt and pepper. Dab with bits of butter, about 2 tsps. per cutlet. Cover dish tightly with foil. Bake 20 to 30 minutes, depending upon thickness of chicken breasts, until chicken is tender when pierced with a knife and white throughout. Juices remaining may be used in soups or sauces.

Skillet-Poached Chicken Breasts

Lay skinned chicken breasts, boneless or with ribs, in a skillet. Add water or broth to just cover chicken. To add flavor, add any of the following — chopped celery, carrot, parsley, garlic, green onion or bouillon. Bring liquid to a boil, reduce heat to a simmer, cover skillet, simmer chicken 8 to 10 minutes if boneless, 12 to 15 minutes with ribs, or until tender. Cool in broth, refrigerate.

Chicken Hurry-Curry

Almost as good as an elaborate chicken curry I make at home. Serve over rice with any traditional curry accompaniments you may have on hand, such as chopped chutney (Major Grey's), diced green peppers, chopped peanuts or cashews, crumbled bacon, chopped scallions.

1 Tbsp. butter
1 Tbsp. curry powder
½ c. milk or half-and-half
1 can condensed cream of chicken soup
1 clove garlic, minced, or 1/8 tsp. garlic powder
1½ to 2 c. diced cooked chicken
(I poach 2 or 3 boneless breast halves)

Melt butter in medium saucepan, add curry powder, stir to blend and cook briefly. Add remaining ingredients, heat through. If needed, add more milk to thin. Serves 2 to 3. *Barbara Tow.*

Chicken and Chiles with Sour Cream

1 3-lb. fryer or 4 half chicken breasts, cooked, cubed
2 cans condensed cream of chicken soup
1 c. sour cream
1 tsp. chili powder
½ tsp. cumin powder
1 bunch green onions, coarsely chopped
2 4-oz. cans green chilies, chopped, drained
12 corn tortillas, torn into bite-size pieces
2 c. grated cheddar cheese

Mix soup, sour cream, chili powder and cumin powder. Spoon half the soup mixture into bottom of baking dish. Layer half of each: chicken, green onions, chilies, tortillas and cheese. Repeat. Bake uncovered in preheated 375-degree oven 30 to 40 minutes or until hot throughout. Serves 4 to 6. Optional side dishes: chopped ripe olives, chopped green onions, salsa. Good with Margaritas, corn, avocado salad.

Cream Sauce for Chicken

A versatile sauce for cooked, chopped chicken. Spoon the creamed chicken into baked Pepperidge Farm patty shells, sprinkle with Parmesan. Or, spoon over noodles, rice, toast or biscuits.

3 Tbsps. butter
3 Tbsps. flour
1½ c. chicken broth
½ c. half-and-half, preferably, or milk
¼ c. snipped parsley
¼ c. chopped scallions
Salt and pepper to taste

Melt butter in large saucepan over medium heat. Add flour slowly, stir constantly a few minutes while flour bubbles and cooks. Gradually add broth and cream or milk, stir constantly until smooth and thickened. Add parsley and scallions, season with salt and pepper. Add chicken, heat through. Thin, if necessary, with broth or cream. 2 cups, serves 4.

Chicken Noodle Casserole

3½ lb. cut-up chicken or 5 half breasts with ribs, cooked, broth reserved
8-oz. pkg. noodles, cooked minimum time
4 Tbsps. butter
1 large onion, chopped
1 c. chopped green pepper
1 c. chopped celery
1 can condensed cream of mushroom soup
1 c. reserved broth
1 c. chopped pimentos (or 1 small jar)
Salt and pepper
1 c. grated cheddar cheese
2 slices bread, buttered, cut in tiny cubes

Sauté onion, peppers and celery in butter to soften. Mix with chicken, noodles and pimentos. Mix soup and broth, add to chicken. Season. Place in baking dish, top with cheese and bread cubes. Bake at 350 degrees about 30 minutes. Serves 6. *C. Ruffenach.*

Chicken and Broccoli Casserole

4 boneless chicken breast halves or 3 chicken breast halves with ribs
1 box frozen chopped broccoli
1 can condensed cream of chicken soup
¼ c. milk
½ c. mayonnaise
1 tsp. lemon juice
¾ tsp. curry powder
Salt and pepper to taste
Parmesan and paprika

Cook chicken, cool, dice. Spoon thawed, very well drained, uncooked broccoli on the bottom of a buttered baking dish. Place sliced or diced chicken over broccoli. Make a sauce of soup, milk, mayonnaise, lemon juice, curry powder, salt and pepper. Smooth over chicken. Sprinkle casserole generously with Parmesan and lightly with paprika. Bake uncovered at 350 degrees, 35 to 40 minutes until hot and browned and puffy on top. Serves 4.

Chicken Alla Francese

4 boneless chicken breast halves
3 Tbsps. flour
Salt and pepper
1 egg, fork-beaten with 1 Tbsp. water
2 Tbsps. olive oil
2 Tbsps. unsalted butter
2 Tbsps. fresh lemon juice
1 Tbsp. fresh chopped parsley or 1 tsp. dried

On a cutting board, flatten chicken gently with the edge of a saucer. Sprinkle both sides with flour, pat on firmly. Season with salt and pepper. Mix egg and water in shallow bowl or pie plate. Dip cutlets in egg, allowing excess to run off. Heat olive oil in a large skillet, sauté chicken over moderate heat 3 to 5 minutes each side. Add butter, lemon juice and parsley to skillet, scraping up browning particles. Spoon sauce over chicken. Serves 4.

Chicken Sauté

4 chicken breasts, with ribs
1 Tbsp. each: oil, butter (more as needed)
Salt and pepper
Dried chervil, tarragon, or other seasoning preferred
1 Tbsp. chopped scallions or 1 tsp. dried chives
1 c. chicken broth
2 Tbsps. butter

Remove skin from chicken, rinse, pat dry. Heat oil and butter in a large skillet. Brown chicken well, both sides. Season with salt and pepper. Sprinkle with chervil, tarragon or other seasoning. Cover, and turning once, cook over low heat about 30 minutes or until chicken is tender when pierced with a fork. Set chicken aside. Add scallions or chives to skillet, stir vigorously to remove all pan drippings. Add broth, boil to reduce liquid by half. Swirl in butter, spoon over chicken. Serves 4. If cooking dark meat with the white, brown dark meat first, cover, cook 5 minutes. Then add breasts to brown. Continue as above.

Chicken and Peppers

4 boneless chicken breast halves
Salt and pepper
1 each: medium red and
    green peppers, thin strips
2 garlic cloves, minced
2 Tbsps. unsalted butter (more if needed)
½ c. broth, bouillon or white wine

Rinse chicken, pat dry, season both sides with salt and pepper. Heat butter in a large skillet over medium heat. Brown chicken, about 3 minutes each side.

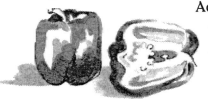

Add pepper strips and garlic. Stirring, cook about 3 minutes. Add liquid, cover, cook over low heat about 5 minutes. Serve peppers and sauce over chicken. Serves 4.

Chicken Alfredo with Asparagus and Linguini

2 boneless chicken breast halves
10 to 12 young fresh asparagus
2 garlic cloves, minced
Dash red pepper flakes
10-oz. carton refrigerated
  prepared Alfredo sauce
  (*e.g.* Contadina)
9-oz. pkg. fresh linguini
  (or substitute dried)
2 Tbsps. olive oil

Slice chicken into strips approximately ½-inch wide by 1½-inches long. Snap off tough ends of asparagus. Cut asparagus into 1½-inch pieces. Mince garlic. Cook linguini as directed. Keep warm. Heat olive oil in a large skillet. When hot, stir-fry chicken about 1 minute. Add asparagus, garlic and pepper flakes. Stir-fry about 2 minutes. (If needed, add a little more olive oil, or butter, while stir-frying.) Drain off excess fat. Reduce heat, add sauce. Stirring, heat mixture until just hot. Serve over hot linguini. Serves 2 to 3.

Chicken Parmesan

4 boneless chicken breast halves
¼ to ½ c. flour, salt and pepper
1 large egg, fork-beaten
1 c. fresh bread crumbs
½ c. Parmesan cheese, grated
2 Tbsps. oil and 4 Tbsps. butter (use less if desired)
Lemon wedges

Dip eggs in seasoned flour, then in egg, then in crumbs mixed with cheese. Heat oil and butter in skillet, cook approximately 6 minutes per side. Serve with lemon wedges. Serves 4.

Chicken Sauté with Curry, Honey and Mustard

4 to 6 boneless chicken breast halves
4 Tbsps. honey
2 Tbsps. Dijon mustard
1 Tbsp. Worcestershire sauce
1½ Tbsps. salad oil
1 tsp. curry powder
1 Tbsp. each: oil, butter

Mix honey, mustard, Worcestershire, oil and curry powder. If there is time, marinate chicken an hour or more. Before cooking, scrape marinade from chicken, reserving marinade. Heat oil and butter in large skillet. Brown chicken over moderate heat. Reduce heat, cook uncovered 20 to 30 minutes basting frequently with marinade. Reserve most of the basting sauce until the chicken is nearly done. Allow to cook at least 5 minutes after final application of marinade. Serves 4, with rice. Or, bake on foil-lined platter at 350 degrees for 20 to 30 minutes. Baste occasionally.

Skillet Chicken Fricassee

4 half chicken breasts with ribs, or other parts, skinned
½ c. flour
salt and pepper
2 Tbsps. salad oil
2 Tbsps. butter
¼ c. dry white wine, chicken broth or bouillon
1 medium onion, cut into thin rings
1 medium green pepper, cut into thin strips
1 medium carrot, thin strips, about 3 in. long
1 stalk celery, thin strips, about 3 in. long
2 cloves garlic, minced
1 c. chicken broth or bouillon

Shake chicken in plastic bag to coat with seasoned flour. Brown chicken in oil and butter in large skillet. Add wine or broth to skillet, scraping up browning particles. Add remaining ingredients, cover skillet, cook on low heat until chicken is tender, about 40 minutes. If sauce is too thin, boil to reduce. Serves 4. Delicious with noodles, rice or potatoes.

Chicken Cacciatore

4 chicken breast halves, or mixed parts, skinned
Salt and pepper
¼ c. olive oil
1 medium onion, sliced into rings
1 green pepper, sliced into rings
2 cloves garlic, chopped
8 large mushrooms, or 1 pint, stemmed, sliced
8-oz. can tomato sauce
14½-oz. can peeled, whole tomatoes, cut up
½ tsp. each: basil, oregano

Season chicken with salt and pepper. Brown in a large skillet in the olive oil over medium-high heat. Set aside. In oil remaining, sauté onion, pepper and garlic about 5 minutes. Add mushrooms, stir and cook about 3 minutes. Set aside. Discard excess oil, scrape up browning particles. Add tomato sauce and tomatoes, cutting tomatoes into small pieces. Add seasonings. Return chicken and vegetables to skillet. Cook, partially covered, 30 to 40 minutes, until chicken is tender. If sauce is too thin, boil vigorously to reduce to desired consistency. Serves 4, with spaghetti or linguini alongside. Pass the Parmesan.

No-Hassle Chicken

2 to 4 chicken breast halves, with ribs, skinned
Salt
Pepper
Garlic powder
1 can cream of chicken or cream of mushroom soup
¾ c. milk or half-and-half

Season chicken with salt, pepper and garlic powder. Place in a baking dish. Cover with soup mixed with milk or half-and-half. Bake uncovered at 325 degrees about 45 minutes or until chicken is tender. Baste occasionally with sauce. May substitute white wine for some of the milk or half-and-half. May add canned or freshly sautéed mushrooms toward end of baking time.

Baked Chicken Parmesan

This is a favorite. May prepare early.

6 Tbsps. butter
4 boneless chicken breast halves
2 or more slices bread for very fine crumbs
¼ c. Parmesan
½ tsp. dry parsley
¼ tsp. garlic powder
Salt and pepper

While preheating oven to 350 degrees, melt butter in the oven in a baking dish. Mix remaining ingredients except chicken. Dip chicken first in melted butter, then in crumbs. Pat on firmly. Place chicken in the baking dish, making sure all the chicken is coated with butter. Sprinkle on any remaining crumbs. Bake uncovered 30 to 45 minutes. Serves 4.

Southern Fried Chicken

Chicken pieces for 4 — drumsticks, breasts and/or thighs
5-oz. can evaporated milk
1 c. flour
Salt and pepper to taste
Salad oil (I use Wesson)

Skin chicken if desired. Rinse, put in large bowl, cover with milk. Soak 15 minutes at room temperature, an hour or longer refrigerated. Put flour, salt and pepper in flat bowl. Drain chicken, roll in flour. Cover completely with a thick layer of flour. Press on firmly. In a large deep pot, heat sufficient oil to cover chicken. When oil is boiling, carefully slip chicken into hot oil. Reduce heat, but keep at a low boil. Cook chicken about 30 minutes, turning frequently. When it is golden brown and tender when pierced with a knife, it is done. Drain on paper towels. Serves 4, hot or cold. *Mrs. Wilkes, adapted.*

Stir-Fry Chicken and Broccoli

2 boneless chicken breast halves, thin strips, 2 inches long
Peanut or salad oil
1 c. small broccoli florets
½ c. sliced fresh mushrooms or sliced
Water chestnuts
4 green onions, 1-inch pieces
2 cloves garlic, minced
Pinch each powdered ginger and red pepper flakes
2 tsps. cornstarch dissolved in ½ c. chicken broth or bouillon
1½ Tbsps. soy sauce
Salt and pepper to taste

Heat 3 Tbsps. oil in a large skillet or wok until hot. Reduce heat slightly, stir-fry chicken about 4 minutes. Set aside. Heat about 2 more Tbsps. oil until hot. Add broccoli, mushrooms or water chestnuts, green onions, garlic, ginger and pepper flakes. Stir-fry about 4 minutes. Return chicken to pan. Stir and heat mixture through. Dissolve cornstarch in broth. Add soy sauce. Stir into chicken until sauce is slightly thickened. Season with salt and pepper. Serves 2, with rice.

Orange and Soy Sauce for Chicken

Use this sauce to baste boneless chicken breasts while sautéing, or baste while baking chicken in 325-degree oven about 30 minutes.

⅓ c. orange juice
2 Tbsps. each: soy sauce, catsup
¼ c. each: sugar, white vinegar, water
1 large clove garlic, minced
1½ Tbsps. cornstarch dissolved in
2 Tbsps. water

Heat ingredients except cornstarch mixture in a small saucepan. Bring to a gentle boil. Reduce heat, add cornstarch mixture, stir just until thickened. About 1 cup.

Baked Chicken and Orange Sauce and Fruit

4 half chicken breasts with ribs, skinned
½ c. flour
Salt and pepper to taste
2 Tbsps each: oil and butter
1½ c. orange juice or drained fruit juice plus orange juice to make 1½ c.
2 Tbsps. each: vinegar, brown sugar
1 tsp. dried basil
½ tsp. nutmeg
15-oz. can peach or apricot halves, drained

Shake chicken in plastic bag with flour, salt and pepper. Brown chicken in oil and butter. Transfer chicken to a baking dish. For sauce, mix juice, vinegar, brown sugar, basil and nutmeg. Pour sauce over chicken. Cover. Bake in 350-degree oven 30 minutes. Uncover. Place drained fruit around chicken. Baste with sauce. Bake uncovered 15 minutes longer or until chicken is tender. If desired, boil pan juices to thicken. Serves 4. *Betsy McBride.*

Chicken and Mushrooms with Buttery Sauce

4 to 6 chicken breast halves with ribs, skinned
1 Tbsp. each: oil and butter
¾ c. uncooked rice, salt and pepper
1 small onion, chopped
3-oz. can mushrooms, undrained
14½-oz. can chicken broth
4 Tbsps. butter
Fresh chopped parsley

Brown chicken in oil and butter. Put rice in oiled baking dish. Season with salt and pepper. Spread onions and mushrooms over rice. Lay chicken over vegetables. Pour broth over all. Dot with butter. Cover (foil is fine), bake at 350 degrees 45 to 60 minutes until chicken is tender and rice is cooked. Sprinkle with parsley if available. Serves 4.

Crispy, Cheesy Chicken Breasts

6 half chicken breasts with ribs, skinned
6 slices Swiss or Edam cheese
1 can cream of chicken soup
¼ c. water
2 c. Pepperidge Farm herb stuffing
½ c. melted butter
¼ c. finely chopped onion

Place chicken in one layer in buttered baking dish or pan. Top each piece of chicken with a slice of cheese. Mix soup and water, pour over chicken. Mix stuffing, butter and onion. Spoon over all. Bake uncovered in 325 degree oven about 1¼ hour or until done. Serves 6. (May use boneless breasts. Bake uncovered 45 to 60 minutes depending upon thickness.)

Easy Chicken a la King

1 can cream of mushroom,
½ c. milk or half-and-half
2 Tbsps. diced pimentos
¼ c. diced green pepper
1 tsp. Worcestershire sauce
1½ c. cubed cooked chicken

Heat soup with milk or half-and-half. Add remaining ingredients, heat through. If desired, add a little more milk to thin. Serve over rice or noodles or in patty shells. Serves 3 or 4.

Notes / Extra Recipes

Arroz Con Pollo (chicken with rice)

4 half chicken breasts, skinned (or parts desired)
Salt, pepper, paprika
3 Tbsps. olive oil
1 medium onion, finely chopped
2 cloves garlic, minced
1 c. uncooked rice
1 medium tomato, cubed
¼ c. chopped parsley
1 bay leaf (remove before serving)
14½-oz. can chicken broth (or 2 c. bouillon)
1 c. frozen peas or 8-oz. can (optional)
2 pimentos, sliced (optional)

Season chicken with salt, pepper and paprika. Heat oil in a large skillet. Brown chicken, about 8 minutes. Add onions, peppers and garlic, stir and cook about 3 minutes. Add remaining ingredients, except peas and pimentos. Cover, cook over low heat until rice is done and chicken is tender, about 45 minutes. Add peas, cook through. Garnish with pimento. Serves 4. Sangria is a good drink with this one-skillet specialty.

Notes / Extra Recipes

Seafood

Jo Gabeler

Seafood

A bonus of boating is the opportunity to enjoy fresh seafood on a regular basis. However, whether the fish is caught by crew members or purchased locally, it should be cooked or frozen promptly. It is also important to avoid overcooking fish. A different variety of fish may be substituted in many of the following recipes. As a general rule, fish which is frozen should be cooked twice as long as unfrozen fish.

Baked Fish with Basting Sauce

A good basic recipe for baking fish is this one from James Beard. There will be about ½ c. of basting sauce sufficient for about 1½ pounds of fillets. Place fish fillets or fish steaks in a foil-lined baking dish or broiler pan. Brush with basting sauce. (I sprinkle with a little paprika, too.) Bake in a preheated 450-degree oven 10 minutes per inch of thickness, measured at the thickest part. Check fillets of ½-inch thickness after 5 minutes. When the fish flakes easily, it is done.

Basting Sauce:
½ c. melted unsalted butter or a mixture of oil and butter
1 tsp. salt
¼ tsp. freshly ground pepper
2 Tbsps. lemon juice

Broiled Flounder Fillets

Allow ⅓ to ½ lb. per person. Preheat broiler. Melt 2 to 3 Tbsps. butter in broiler pan large enough to hold fillets in one layer. Lay fish in pan skin side down, season with salt and pepper, coat with butter. Sprinkle about 2 Tbsps. fine fresh bread crumbs over fish, dust very lightly with paprika. Broil about 5 inches from heat source 3 to 5 minutes. Garnish with lemon wedges. Serves 2.

Baked Flounder with Chili Butter

Bland flounder becomes more assertive with peppy seasonings.

2 flounder fillets, about 1/3 lb. each
3 Tbsps. butter
¼ tsp. chili powder, more if desired
Generous pinch each: cayenne, cumin powder and garlic powder

Preheat oven to 475 degrees. Melt butter in oven in a shallow baking pan which will hold fillets in a single layer. Be careful that butter does not burn. Mix seasonings with melted butter. Lay fish in pan skin side down. Brush with seasoned butter. Bake in mid-oven 3 to 5 minutes without turning the fillets. Serves 2.

Baked Grouper

Disposable foil pans are handy for dipping and baking.

2 grouper fillets (or other firm-fleshed fish)
1 egg, fork-beaten with 1 Tbsp. water
Salt and pepper
2 slices of bread for fine crumbs (about 1 c.)
3 Tbsps. melted butter
Paprika

Preheat oven to 400 degrees. Mix egg and water in shallow pan or pie plate, add salt and pepper. Place crumbs in a second pan. Rinse fillets, wipe dry, dip in egg mixture. Let excess drip off, then dip in crumbs to coat well on both sides. Dust lightly with paprika. Place in oiled baking pan. Drizzle with butter. Bake in mid-oven an average of 8 minutes, until fish flakes easily when tested with the tines of a fork. Serve with lemon wedges and tartar sauce.

Baked Fish Mexican Style

A Diane Rollings' specialty from Hey Jose Restaurant in Provo.

1¼ to 1½ lbs. boneless fish fillets or fish steaks about ¾-inch thick
1 c. tomato-based salsa (I use Pace Picante Sauce, medium hot)
1 c. shredded sharp Cheddar cheese
½ c. coarsely crushed corn chips
Lime wedges

Rinse fish, pat dry, place pieces side by side in a baking dish. Spoon salsa over fish, sprinkle evenly with cheese, then with the corn chips. Bake uncovered in preheated 400-degree oven until fish is just done, about 12 to 15 minutes. Serve with lime wedges, and, if desired, garnish with avocado slices and sour cream. Serves 4.

Fabulous Baked Fish

5-oz. can evaporated milk (no substitution)
1 egg
1 tsp. salt
½ tsp. pepper
4 to 6 boneless, mild-flavored fish fillets, ⅓ to ½ lb. each
1 c. unseasoned bread crumbs (fresh preferred)
About 2 Tbsps. melted butter
Lemon wedges

Whisk together milk, egg, salt and pepper. Marinate fish fillets about 15 minutes. Meanwhile, preheat oven to 500 degrees. Oil a shallow baking pan. Lift fillets from milk, let excess milk drip off fish, coat with crumbs. Arrange on baking sheet. Drizzle with melted butter, bake in upper part of oven 10 to 15 minutes, depending upon thickness of fish. Serves 4 to 6. *Dixie Crystals, Savannah.*

Broiled Grouper with Mustard and Onions

Approximately ⅔ lb. grouper (or other white fish) fillet
1 Tbsp. olive oil
1 Tbsp. butter
1½ Tbsps. grainy Dijon mustard
½ c. coarsely chopped onions (1 small onion)
Salt and pepper

Mix olive oil, butter (softened), mustard and onions. Season fish with salt and pepper. Place in shallow baking pan (foil will do) or broiler pan. Spread mustard mixture over fish. Preheat oven to broil. Broil fish in mid-oven approximately 10 minutes. Test after 8 minutes. It is done when fish flakes easily when tested with a fork. Serves 2.

Fish Fillets with Lemon-Caper Sauce

The fillets should sizzle briskly the entire time they are cooking. While the butter will brown, take care that it does not burn and blacken.

4 flounder (or other fish) fillets (1½ lbs.)
Salt
Pepper
Flour
2 Tbsps. salad oil
2 Tbsps. unsalted butter
Juice of 1 large lemon
1 (additional) Tbsp. butter
1 Tbsp. drained capers

Rinse fillets quickly in cold water, pat dry. Season liberally with salt and coarsely ground pepper. Dredge in flour. Heat oil and butter in large heavy skillet on medium-high until butter sizzles. Cook fish at medium-high on one side about 3 minutes until browned and crispy. Turn fish, cook on second side about 3 minutes or until done. Turn fish only once. Remove to serving platter or plates. Lower heat, melt additional butter, add lemon juice and capers, sizzle 1 minute. Pour over fish and serve immediately. Serves 4. *Martha Nesbit, Savannah.*

Breaded Fish Fillets

1½ lbs. skinned fish fillets
¾ c. flour
Salt, pepper
1 egg
1 tsp. oil
1 Tbsp. water
¾ c. (more if needed) fine fresh bread crumbs
3 Tbsps. salad oil
1 Tbsp. butter

Rinse fish, blot dry. Dip into flour mixed with salt and pepper. Beat egg with oil and water. Dip fish in egg wash. Coat with crumbs, pressing on firmly. Heat oil and butter over medium-high heat. When hot, add fish. Turning once, cook about 5 minutes for thin fillets, 10 to 12 minutes for thicker fillets. Serves 4.

Pan-Broiled Salmon Fillet

Boneless salmon sufficient for 2
Olive oil
¼ c. honey
½ tsp. chili powder
1 clove garlic, minced
Lemon or lime wedges

Mix together honey, chili powder and garlic. Over medium-high heat, warm a heavy skillet until hot. Brush with olive oil, about a capful or two. Cook salmon approximately 3 minutes per side until light pink throughout but still firm. Just before fish is done, add honey mixture, let it bubble vigorously, serve over fish. Pass lemon or lime wedges. *S. Elkind.*

Herb Baked Salmon

2 salmon steaks or fillets
¾ c. milk or half-and-half
1 tsp. fresh minced dill or chopped chives
Salt and pepper

Preheat oven to 350 degrees. Place salmon in a shallow baking dish. Add half-and-half or milk to half the depth of the salmon. Sprinkle with seasonings. Basting occasionally, bake about 30 minutes or until salmon is pink throughout. *Helen Gustafson, adapted.*

Cajun Fish

2 Tbsps. butter
About ¾ lb. boneless fish fillets
Cajun seasoning to taste
About ¼ c. fine fresh breadcrumbs

Preheat oven to 350 degrees. Melt butter in shallow baking pan. Rinse fish, blot dry, dip in butter to coat both sides. Sprinkle lightly with Cajun Seasoning. Sprinkle with a light coating of bread crumbs. Bake uncovered without turning an average of 8 minutes, or until fish flakes when tested with fork. Serves 2.

My Cajun Seasoning

2 tsps. paprika
½ tsp. each: garlic powder, white pepper, cayenne
¼ tsp. each: salt, thyme, oregano
⅛ tsp. coarse ground black pepper

Store in covered bottle, use sparingly to flavor any bland-tasting fish. (Good for chicken and pork, too.)

Baked Fish with Diced Vegetables and Lemon

Brush baking pan with olive oil. Brush fish fillets with olive oil. Season with salt and pepper or a fish seasoning mix. Dice a tomato or two, 4 to 6 green onions and a clove of garlic. Make a shallow bed of vegetables for the fillets to rest on. Squeeze on juice of half a lemon. Bake in preheated 350-degree oven until fish is done, about 10 minutes for each inch of thickness measured at thickest part.

All-Purpose Seasoning for Fish

1 Tbsp. dried parsley
1 tsp. onion powder
1 tsp. garlic powder
½ tsp. dill weed
½ tsp. paprika, salt
Pinch of pepper

Store in tightly-covered spice bottle.

Crab Soufflé

8 slices thin, firm white bread (Pepperidge Farm)
1 lb. lump crabmeat, all shell removed
½ c. mayonnaise
1 medium onion, chopped
1 c. each, chopped: celery, green pepper
4 eggs
3 c. milk
1 can cream of mushroom soup
½ c. grated Cheddar cheese

Dice 4 slices bread. Put into bottom of a large buttered casserole dish. Gently, without breaking up crabmeat too much, mix crab, mayonnaise, onion, celery and green pepper. Spread over bread. Trim crust from the remaining 4 slices of bread. Dice and distribute over crab. Mix eggs, milk and soup. Pour over all. Refrigerate several hours or overnight. Top with cheese before baking, uncovered, in preheated 350 degree oven for 1 hour. Serves 6 to 8. Nice for brunch, for a summer supper or as the seafood dish at a buffet. (May substitute chicken for the crabmeat.)

Crabmeat and Artichoke Casserole

1 lb. crabmeat, all shell removed
14-oz. can artichoke hearts or 1 box frozen, cooked
4 hard-boiled eggs, sliced
3 Tbsps. each: butter, flour
1½ to 2 c. milk or cream
1 tsp. salt
½ tsp. each: dry mustard, Worcestershire
Pepper and Tabasco to taste
¼ c. Parmesan
½ c. buttered bread crumbs
Additional ¼ c. Parmesan

Slice artichokes in halves or quarters. Arrange on bottom of shallow baking dish. Arrange sliced eggs over them. Make a white sauce by melting butter, stirring in flour, cooking a few minutes, then adding, while stirring over medium heat, milk or cream to desired consistency. Add seasonings and ¼ c. Parmesan. Fold in crabmeat, spoon over artichokes. Top with breadcrumbs, then Parmesan. Bake at 350 degrees until hot throughout, about 35 minutes if made ahead and coming from refrigerator. Serves 6. *Lorie Burch.*

Easy Crab Cakes

1 lb. fresh crabmeat, shell removed
Salt, pepper, dash cayenne
2 Tbsps. chopped fresh parsley
¾ c. fine fresh bread crumbs
2 eggs, fork-beaten
1 tsp. Worcestershire sauce
4 Tbsps. unsalted butter

Mix crabmeat with remaining ingredients except butter. Press out excess moisture while making 6 to 8 crab cakes. Heat butter in large skillet, cook crab cakes over moderate heat until hot throughout and golden brown on both sides, 8 to 10 minutes. Serve with tartar sauce and lemon wedges. Serves 4 to 6. (If desired, cover crab with fine fresh bread crumbs before cooking.)

Crab Imperial

Nice for entertaining. May make ahead.

2 Tbsps. butter
1 clove garlic, minced
1 c. finely chopped celery
⅓ c. minced onion
1 Tbsp. finely chopped green pepper
2 (additional) Tbsps. butter
3 Tbsps. flour
1 c. milk
½ c. Hellman's mayonnaise
½ tsp. curry powder
2 Tbsps. lemon juice
Salt to taste, dash Tabasco
1 lb. fresh lump crabmeat
Tiny buttered bread cubes
Paprika

Sauté vegetables in butter in skillet until softened. Make a white sauce (thick) of butter, flour and milk. Stir in mayonnaise and the seasonings. Fold in crabmeat and vegetables. Spoon into 8 x 8-inch baking dish, top with bread cubes, sprinkle with paprika, bake uncovered in preheated 350-degree oven about 30 minutes. Serves 4. May cook in shells 15 minutes.

Deviled Crab

1 lb. lump crabmeat, shell removed
1½ Tbsps. butter
⅓ c. chopped onions
⅓ c. chopped celery
⅓ c. chopped scallions
⅓ c. chopped peppers
½ c. mayonnaise
1 Tbsp. Dijon mustard
1 tsp. Worcestershire sauce
½ c. fine fresh bread crumbs
2 Tbsps. chopped parsley
Salt and freshly ground black pepper
Additional 1 c. bread crumbs
Additional 1½ Tbsps. butter, melted

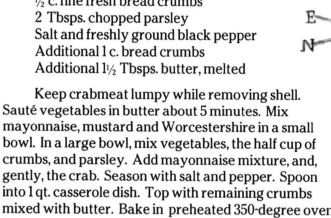

Keep crabmeat lumpy while removing shell. Sauté vegetables in butter about 5 minutes. Mix mayonnaise, mustard and Worcestershire in a small bowl. In a large bowl, mix vegetables, the half cup of crumbs, and parsley. Add mayonnaise mixture, and, gently, the crab. Season with salt and pepper. Spoon into 1 qt. casserole dish. Top with remaining crumbs mixed with butter. Bake in preheated 350-degree oven about 30 minutes. Serves 4. *Marian Morash, adapted.* (May bake in four 5-inch scallop shells for less time.)

Canned Crabmeat

May be improved by rinsing, draining very well, and tossing with a bit of lemon juice and olive oil. Crown Prince is a popular brand.

Steamed Crabs

Place a steamer rack in bottom of a large pot. Bring a few inches of water to a boil in the pot. Add 1 tsp. salt. Add crabs. Steam, covered, 15 to 20 minutes or until red. Remove crabs. Rinse with cold water. Cool to room temperature.

SCALLOPS should be cooked within 2 days after purchasing. Quite bland and only slightly sweet, scallops can be a joy for the imaginative cook. Whether sautéed, baked, broiled or grilled, they should never be overcooked or they will turn tasteless and tough. Since scallops cook quickly, it is advisable to bring them to room temperature before cooking so they will be warm throughout.

Less often available, deluxe bay scallops are the little ones. Sea scallops, the bigger ones, are usually less expensive but sometimes are more flavorful. When a scallop is more than an inch across, slice it in half crosswise.

Scallops give off considerable moisture, so they should be blotted dry with paper towels after rinsing. When they are floured, take care not to add too many scallops to the skillet at one time, or excess moisture may turn the flour gummy.

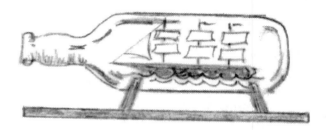

Broiled Scallops

1½ pints scallops, halved if large
½ c. milk
1½ c. fresh bread crumbs
Salt, freshly ground pepper
1 stick unsalted butter, melted
1 Tbsp. finely chopped parsley
Lemon wedges and tartar sauce

Rinse scallops, drain, dry completely with paper towels. Dip in milk, roll lightly in crumbs. Arrange in a shallow pan, sprinkle with salt and pepper. Spoon 4 Tbsps. butter over scallops. Broil in preheated oven 4 inches from heat just until crumbs are lightly browned, about 5 minutes. Pour on remaining butter mixed with parsley. Serve with lemon wedges and tartar sauce. Serves 4.

Coquilles St. Jacques (scallops in shells)

4 bsps. butter
1 c. fresh mushroom slices
¼ c. minced scallions
2 cloves garlic, minced
Salt and pepper
½ c. chopped parsley
1 c. fine fresh bread crumbs
1 pint bay scallops
4 (additional) Tbsps. butter

Melt butter in a small skillet. Stirring, cook mushrooms until softened. Add scallions and garlic, cook a few more minutes, stirring. Mix parsley, bread crumbs and scallops gently in a medium bowl. Add cooled mushroom mixture. Spoon mixture into 6 buttered scallop shells (or a shallow baking dish). Drizzle with melted butter. Bake in preheated 450-degree oven 10 minutes. Broil quickly to brown. Serves 6.

Scallops Amandine

½ to ¾ lb. scallops, halved if large
¼ c. flour, salt to taste
4 Tbsps. butter, divided
1 Tbsp. oil
3 Tbsps. slivered almonds
1 Tbsp. lemon juice
2 Tbsps. fresh chopped parsley

Blot scallops dry, dredge in flour with salt. Heat 2 Tbsps. butter and 1 Tbsp. oil in large skillet. Over moderately high heat, sauté scallops (keeping them separated) until browned and cooked, about 4 minutes. Remove with slotted spoon, cover to keep warm. Heat additional 2 Tbsps. butter, brown almonds quickly, stir in lemon juice and parsley, spoon over scallops. Serves 2.

Stir-Fry Scallops

Rinse and dry scallops. Heat a few Tbsps. olive oil in skillet or wok until hot. Sear ½ lb. scallops quickly. Add 1 small tomato, diced, 1 garlic clove, minced, 2 chopped green onions, and, if desired, diced zucchini. Season with salt, pepper and basil. Stir-fry about 3 minutes. Sprinkle with lemon juice. Present with pasta or rice. Serves 2.

Baked Oysters

2 Tbsps. butter
1 c. fine fresh bread crumbs
1 tsp. finely chopped garlic
2 Tbsps. fresh chopped parsley
2 doz. fresh oysters
3 Tbsps. Parmesan cheese
2 (additional) Tbsps. butter

Melt the 2 Tbsps. butter in a skillet. Add crumbs and garlic, toss over moderate heat a few minutes until golden. Stir in parsley. Spread ⅔ c. in bottom of buttered baking dish, about 7 x 11 inches. Place oysters over crumbs in a single layer. Mix crumbs remaining with Parmesan. Spread over oysters. Dot with bits of butter. Bake in preheated 425-degree oven about 15 minutes. Serves 4.

Oysters

Scrub shells with a stiff brush under cold running water. Place cupped sides down on a cutting board. Force a strong, narrow-bladed knife into the curved side opposite the hinge. Cut all the way around until the muscle is severed. Pull off the top shell, loosen or remove the oyster in the bottom shell.

Scalloped Oysters

1 pint fresh oysters, drained (reserve oyster liquor)
½ c. melted butter
½ c. fine bread crumbs
1 c. cracker crumbs
Salt and pepper to taste
3 Tbsps. oyster liquor
1 Tbsp. milk

Preheat oven to 450 degrees. Mix butter, bread crumbs, cracker crumbs. Spread ⅓ of crumb mixture over bottom of a small baking dish. Add a layer of half the oysters. Season with salt and pepper. Mix oyster liquor and milk. Spoon half over the oysters. Add another ⅓ of crumbs, then remaining oysters and liquid remaining. Top casserole with remaining crumbs. Bake for 30 minutes. Serves 4.

Fried Oysters

Drain oysters, rinse, blot dry. Dip in egg whipped with a little salt and pepper. Roll in bread crumbs or cracker crumbs. Heat enough oil to cover oysters in a skillet. When hot, fry oysters 2 to 3 minutes. Drain on paper towels.

Boiled Lobster

A 1½-lb. lobster will yield about 6 ozs. of lobster meat. The most popular size lobster to buy weighs 1½ to 2 lbs. Fill a big pot (*e.g.*, 15 to 18-qt. "lobster" pot) about ⅔ full with water, adding about 1 Tbsp. salt for each gallon of water. Bring to a rolling boil. Rinse lobsters, drop head first into the pot. Cover pot, return water to a boil, reduce heat until water is boiling gently. Cook a 1½ lb. lobster 15 minutes, a 1 lb. lobster 10 minutes, a 2 lb. lobster 20 minutes. Drain cooking water. Hold lobster upside down to drain lobster.

Linguini with Clam Sauce

2 Tbsps. olive oil
2 cloves garlic, minced
¼ c. dry white wine
2 6½-oz. cans chopped clams, liquor reserved
½ c. fresh chopped parsley
1 tsp. dried basil
Salt and pepper, freshly-ground preferred
8 ozs. linguini

Heat the oil in a medium saucepan, cook garlic a few minutes, stirring. Add wine and the liquor from the 2 cans of clams. Add parsley and basil, season with salt and pepper. Simmer about 15 minutes, add clams, heat through. Serve over hot linguini. 2 generous servings

Steamed Clams

Scrub clams under cold running water with a stiff brush or old toothbrush. Put them into a pot. (They may be placed in a colander or steamer first, but it is not essential.) Add water, or white wine, or a combination to a depth of 1 inch. Bring the liquid to a boil, reduce heat, cover pot, steam clams over low heat until they open, 5 to 10 minutes. Discard unopened clams. Put clams on a plate, strain cooking broth into a bowl, served melted butter or lemon butter in a second bowl. Dip a clam in broth to rinse, then in butter. May serve cocktail sauce, too. Allow about 8 cherrystone clams per person or 1 lb. of steamers.

Fried Clams

24 shucked clams, halved
1 egg, 1 Tbsp. milk, salt and pepper
1 c. fine dry bread crumbs

Drain clams, dip in egg wash, roll in crumbs. Fry in skillet in hot oil until golden brown, just a few minutes. Serves 4. Offer with cocktail sauce, tartar sauce and/or lemon wedges.

Boiled Shrimp

While it is not essential to devein shrimp, I always do it for aesthetic reasons and because the vein is often gritty. If shrimp has been shelled before cooking, reduce the cooking time by about half. Shelled or not, it is very important not to overcook shrimp.

1 lb. unpeeled shrimp
1 Tbsp. salt
2 qts. water

Bring salted water to a boil. Add shrimp, return to a boil. Reduce heat. Cook medium shrimp uncovered about 5 minutes, small shrimp less time, large shrimp a little longer. A shrimp is done when the center is opaque. Shell and devein.

Crispy Fried Shrimp

¾ lb. shrimp, shelled, deveined, blotted dry
1 egg
1 Tbsp. oil
⅓ c. ice water
½ c. flour
½ tsp. salt
Oil for frying (Wesson recommended)

Whisk egg until frothy in medium-size bowl. Stir in oil, water, flour and salt. If possible, let batter rest an hour or more, covered, so flour particles will expand and batter will thicken. In medium skillet, heat sufficient oil to cover shrimp in a single layer. Add shrimp to batter. Lift shrimp from batter with tongs or a slotted spoon. Let excess batter drip off before adding several shrimp at a time to hot oil. (Do not add too many at a time, or oil will cool down too much.) Stirring constantly, cook shrimp an average of 5 minutes. Remove as done to paper towels, cover with foil to keep warm. Serves 2. Use the same amount of batter for 4.

Scampi

4 Tbsps. unsalted butter
1½ to 2 lbs. large shrimp, shelled, deveined
Salt and pepper to taste
3 cloves garlic, finely minced
¼ c. fresh chopped parsley
3 Tbsps. fresh lemon juice

Heat butter over moderate heat
in large skillet. Add shrimp. Stirring, cook
about 5 minutes. Add garlic, stir-fry a little longer. Season with salt and pepper.
Stir in parsley and lemon juice. Serves 4. Excellent over rice.

Broiled Scampi

¾ lb. medium or large shrimp
3 Tbsps. each: butter, olive oil
2 tsps. lemon juice
2 Tbsps. chopped green onions
1 tsp. or more minced garlic
Fresh chopped parsley
Lemon wedges

Shell and devein shrimp, blot
dry. Preheat broiler. Melt butter in
shallow baking dish or broiler pan.
Do not brown. Mix in olive oil, lemon
juice, green onions and garlic. Place
shrimp in dish in one layer, stir to coat with butter. Sprinkle with salt and
pepper. Broil about 4 inches from heat source about 5 minutes. Turn, broil 3 to 5
minutes longer until shrimp are lightly browned and cooked through. Sprinkle
with parsley, garnish with lemon wedges. Serves 2.

NOTE: Take care not to overcook the shrimp. We like this
shrimp over rice, linguini or angel hair pasta. If not serving over
rice or pasta, you may cut down on the amount of oil and butter
used for broiling.

Shrimp Pilaf

2¼ lbs. shrimp, shelled, deveined
8 slices bacon
2 Tbsps. bacon fat
1 c. chopped onion
½ c. chopped green pepper
½ c. chopped scallions
1½ c. uncooked rice
28-oz. can tomatoes, crushed with juices
Seasonings to taste: salt, pepper, cayenne, Worcestershire, Tabasco,
    lemon juice, thyme, parsley
Chopped parsley

Refrigerate shelled shrimp until time to cook. Cook bacon until crisp, drain on paper towel. Chop coarsely, set aside. Heat bacon fat in large skillet. Sauté vegetables only briefly. Stir in rice, add tomatoes. Season to taste carefully. It should be "hot", but not too "hot". Cover, cook until rice is nearly done, about 15 minutes. Check seasonings. Add shrimp. Stirring occasionally, cook until shrimp are done, 5 to 10 minutes. If mixture is too dry, add a little tomato juice, tomato sauce or water. Top with chopped parsley and crumbled bacon. Serves 6.

Garlic Shrimp Stir-Fry

¾ lb. shrimp, shelled, deveined
2 Tbsps. olive oil
2 cloves garlic, minced
2 Tbsps. each: shallots and scallions,
    chopped, or 4 chopped scallions
Pinch crushed red pepper flakes
Salt and pepper to taste
1 Tbsp. chopped fresh parsley or 1 tsp. dried
1 Tbsp. lemon juice

Heat oil in skillet or wok until hot. Add remaining ingredients except lemon juice. Stir-fry about 5 minutes. Add lemon juice. May add some chopped red or green peppers. Serves 2 with rice.

Shrimp Chow Mein

½ lb. shrimp, shelled, deveined
2 Tbsps. peanut or vegetable oil
1 c. shredded cabbage
½ c. diagonally-sliced celery
1 small onion, thinly sliced, slices halved
2 cloves garlic, minced
4 water chestnuts, sliced
1 Tbsp. or more soy sauce
½ c. chicken broth or bouillon
1 Tbsp. cornstarch dissolved in 2 Tbsps. water

Heat oil in large skillet or wok. When hot, add shrimp, stir-fry 2 minutes. Remove with slotted spoon, set aside. Add cabbage, celery, onion, garlic and water chestnuts, cook, stirring, over medium-high heat 3 minutes. Return shrimp to pan, season with soy sauce. Stir in cornstarch mixture, stir until slightly thickened. Offer with rice. Serves 2.

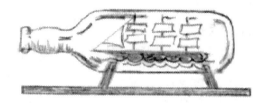

Baked Lemon Shrimp with Garlic

About ⅔ lb. large shrimp (about 6 per serving)
1 stick unsalted butter
½ tsp. salt
1 to 2 cloves garlic, minced
¼ c. fresh chopped parsley, divided
1 Tbsp. grated lemon peel (zest)
1 T bsp. fresh lemon juice, or to taste

Peel and devein shrimp. Melt butter with salt in an ovenproof shallow baking dish in preheated 450 degree oven. Stir in garlic and half the parsley. Add shrimp, bake 5 minutes. Turn. Sprinkle with remaining parsley, the lemon zest and lemon juice. Bake until shrimp are cooked, 5 to 10 minutes more. Garnish with lemon wedges. Serves 2. *Gail Zweigenthal, Editor, Gourmet Magazine, adapted.*

Seafood Gumbo

A treat best made at home to take aboard.

¼ c. each: bacon fat, Wesson oil
½ c. flour
1½ c. fresh okra, chopped (or 1 box frozen, thawed)
½ c. each, chopped: celery, green pepper
1 c. chopped onion
1 clove garlic, minced
8-oz. bottle clam juice
2 14½-oz. cans chicken broth (may want more)
2 bay leaves
1 tsp. salt
¼ tsp. each: cayenne, crumbled thyme
1 lb. crabmeat, picked over
1½ lbs. shrimp, shelled, deveined
12-oz. container fresh oysters

Heat bacon fat and oil in iron skillet, or large pot, until hot. Stir in flour, cook over low heat, stirring frequently until nut-brown. (Be patient, as this is a very important step in making the roux.) Add chopped vegetables, sauté in roux until softened. Transfer to pot. Add heated clam juice and broth. (Heating prevents the roux and vegetables from turning gummy.) Add seasonings. Simmer about 30 minutes to blend flavors. Add shrimp, cook through. Add crab and oysters. Simmer until hot. Spoon over mounds of rice. Serves 8.

Shrimp Boil

2 lbs. medium or large shrimp in the shell
Water or beer in a large pot to cover shrimp
2 large cloves of garlic, peeled
3 whole allspice (optional)
1 tsp. each: red pepper flakes, peppercorns, salt
1 bay leaf
1 each, sliced: onion, lemon

Bring water or beer to a boil with all the ingredients except shrimp. Simmer 10 minutes to blend flavors. Add shrimp, return to a boil, reduce heat, cook about 5 minutes. Drain, serve on newspapers. Diners peel their own. Serves 4. Try lemon butter for dipping.

Shrimp Puff

1 lb. shrimp, cooked, shelled, deveined
6 slices firm white bread, crusts trimmed, lightly buttered
½ lb. sharp cheddar cheese, grated (2 c. grated)
3 eggs, beaten
½ tsp. each: dry mustard, salt
Dash each: pepper, paprika
2 c. milk

Cut shrimp into 2 or 3 pieces. Cut bread into small cubes. Put half the bread cubes into a buttered baking dish, about 7 x 11 inches. Cover with half the shrimp, then half the cheese. Repeat. Mix eggs, seasonings and milk. Pour over all. Cover, refrigerate overnight. Bake uncovered in 325-degree oven about 50 minutes until puffy and golden brown. Serves 4 to 6.

Shrimp and Artichoke Casserole

1 lb. shrimp, cooked, deveined
½ lb. fresh mushrooms, sliced
2 Tbsps. butter
10-oz. pkg. frozen artichokes, thawed, halved
4 Tbsps. butter
2½ Tbsps. flour
1½ c. half-and-half
1 Tbsp. Worcestershire sauce
¼ c. dry sherry
½ tsp salt
¼ tsp. pepper
⅛ tsp. cayenne pepper
½ c. Parmesan cheese, paprika

Arrange artichoke hearts in buttered baking dish, about 11 x 7 inches. Cover with shrimp. Sauté mushrooms in 2 T. butter. Drain, spoon over shrimp. Melt 4 T. butter in a saucepan. Add flour, stir and cook a few minutes. Slowly add half-and-half, stirring constantly until sauce is smooth and thick. Remove from heat, stir in Worcestershire, sherry and seasonings. Pour sauce over shrimp. Sprinkle with Parmesan, and, lightly, with paprika. Bake uncovered in preheated 355 degree oven about 30 minutes or until hot. Serves 4. We serve it with rice mixed with fresh chopped parsley and a tossed green salad. May substitute canned artichokes.

Meats &
Grilled Foods

The Grill

*G*rilled food tastes delicious on the boat, and cooking outside means a cooler galley. While many boat grills use propane, other grills use charcoal. And sometimes the crew goes ashore with a hibachi or to use grills or fireplaces ashore. So, we don't need soggy charcoal. Keep that charcoal dry by putting the paper-wrapped bags of charcoal into plastic bags. Also, keep a spray bottle of water nearby for dousing flames.

When basting foods with their marinades, heed the food safety warning to cook the foods at least 5 minutes after the final basting. Also, never cut cooked meat or poultry on a cutting board which was used to cut the uncooked meat or chicken.

A Basic Marinade

Can be made anytime by mixing a simple vinaigrette — 2 or 3 parts oil to 1 part vinegar or lemon juice. Enhance with seasonings which flatter the foods.

Barbecue Sauce with Chili Powder

¼ c. brown sugar
¼ c. Worcestershire sauce
¼ c. red wine vinegar, water
¼ c. catsup
1 tsp. chili powder.

Use to marinate and baste beef or pork.

Good Southern Barbecue Sauce

¾ c. catsup
⅓ c. cider vinegar
1 Tbsp. Worcestershire sauce
¼ to ½ tsp. liquid smoke
2 Tbsps. brown sugar
1 tsp. paprika
¼ tsp. garlic powder

For steak, burgers, chicken, pork. *Savannah Gas.*

Mary Lou's Barbecue Sauce

2 Tbsps. salad oil
½ c. finely chopped onion
1 clove garlic, minced
½ c. each: honey, catsup, red wine vinegar
¼ c. Worcestershire sauce
1½ tsps. dry mustard
¾ sp. salt
½ tsp. oregano
¼ tsp. thyme
¼ black pepper

Sauté onions and garlic in oil to soften. Add remaining ingredients. Simmer about 30 minutes. About 1½ cups. Delicious on hamburgers, steak, spareribs and pork chops.

Honey Mustard Glaze

A nice finishing sauce with Oriental overtones. Good for chicken, pork and ham.

2 Tbsps. soy sauce
2 Tbsps. dry mustard
1 Tbsp. cider vinegar
6 Tbsps. honey

Stir to blend. Brush on chops, ribs, ham or chicken near end of grilling time. *L. Bloom.*

Lemon Marinade for Chicken

This is our family's favorite chicken marinade.

¼ c. salad oil
½ c. fresh lemon juice
2 cloves garlic, minced
½ tsp. salt
¼ tsp. pepper
¼ tsp. thyme

Marinate skinned chicken pieces in a zip-lock bag several hours if possible. Drain before grilling, baste with marinade. Serves 4.

Paprika Marinade for Chicken

½ c. salad oil (part may be olive oil)
½ c. lemon juice
2 Tbsps. Worcestershire sauce
1 Tbsp. vinegar
Dash Tabasco sauce
1 Tbsp. paprika
1 tsp. each: salt, sugar
¼ tsp. garlic powder

Whisk ingredients to blend thoroughly. Marinate chicken several hours if possible. Drain off marinade, use for basting. About 1 cup.

Hot Deviled Pork Chops

¼ c. catsup
2 Tbsps. each: water, red wine vinegar
1 Tbsp. each: Worcestershire, sugar
½ Tbsp. dry mustard
¼ tsp. each: salt, black pepper
Pinch crushed red pepper flakes
1 onion, sliced
1 slice lemon

Simmer to blend flavors. Use hot or cold. Baste while grilling chops.

Easy Marinade for Pork

½ c. chili sauce
¼ c. lemon juice
2 Tbsps. Worcestershire sauce

Mix well, baste with marinade while grilling

Herb Marinade for Pork

1 c. salad oil
¼ c. white vinegar
½ tsp. each: thyme, tarragon, parsley
¼ tsp. each: salt, pepper

Mix well, baste with marinade while grilling.

Pineapple Sauce for Pork

Good for pork chops, pork tenderloin or kebabs. Basting sauce with honey or brown sugar can burn quickly, so baste toward the end of the grilling time and watch carefully.

2 Tbsps. each: honey, mustard, brown sugar,
Worcestershire sauce
¼ c. pineapple juice
⅓ c. white vinegar
⅛ to ¼ tsp. Tabasco sauce

Mix ingredients to make about 1 cup.

Pork Kebabs

Alternate cubes of boneless pork with green and/or red pepper sections and onion slices. Canned pineapple chunks are good, too. We heat them on a separate skewer since they only need heating through. Juice from the canned pineapple may be used in the sauce (above).

Glazing Mixture for Pork or Ham

5 Tbsps. Dijon mustard
1 Tbsp. honey
3 Tbsps. brown sugar
¾ c. apricot or pineapple preserves

Brush on toward end of grilling time.

Lemon Marinade for Pork

½ tsp. salt
⅛ tsp. pepper
3 Tbsps. lemon juice,
3 Tbsps. olive oil
3 parsley sprigs
¼ tsp. thyme or sage
1 bay leaf
1 clove mashed garlic

Rub salt and pepper into meat. Mix remaining ingredients in a bowl. Marinate pork covered, several hours if possible. Turn occasionally.

Lamb Chops

    4 to 6 thick lamb chops, trimmed of fat
    ¼ c. salad oil
    2 Tbsps. fresh lemon juice
    ½ tsp. salt
    ⅛ tsp. pepper
    1 large clove garlic, minced

  Mix ingredients for marinade. Marinate chops several hours if possible. Drain off marinade before cooking. Use to baste while grilling. (A favorite.)

Rosemary Marinade for Lamb

    ¼ c. olive oil
    2 Tbsps. red wine vinegar
    1 clove garlic, minced
    ½ tsp. crushed rosemary
    ¼ tsp. each: cayenne pepper, paprika

  Mix ingredients. Marinate lamb for several hours.

Herb Marinade for Lamb

    ½ c. salad oil
    ½ c. chopped onion
    ¼ c. chopped parsley
    ¼ c. lemon juice
    1 tsp. each: thyme, marjoram
    ½ tsp. each: salt, pepper
    1 clove garlic, minced

  Mix ingredients to marinate 2 lbs. boneless lamb for kebabs. Thread lamb on 6 skewers with onion and green and red pepper sections. Grill about 12 minutes basting with marinade. Serves 6.

Easy Marinade for Steak

    ½ c. Italian salad dressing
    2 Tbsps. each: soy sauce, Worcestershire sauce
    1 clove garlic, minced

  Marinate for 1 hour. Sufficient for steaks for 4.

Grilled Flank Steak

1½ lbs. flank steak
2 Tbsps. soy sauce
1½ Tbsps. honey
1 Tbsp. vinegar
¾ tsp. garlic powder
¾ tsp. ground ginger
6 Tbsps. salad oil
1 green onion, finely chopped

Marinate steak covered in a shallow dish 2 to 8 hours. Turn occasionally. Grill to medium-rare. Slice thinly across the grain. *Phebe Downey.*

Beef Shish Kebabs

Quantities of vegetables may be varied.

2½ lbs. boneless sirloin or tenderloin, 1½ to 2-inch cubes
2 medium onions, halved, layers separated
2 green peppers, 2-inch pieces
1 pint cherry tomatoes or 4 firm tomatoes, cut into wedges
1 pint large mushrooms, stemmed
Any oil and vinegar dressing or melted garlic butter for basting

Alternate cubes of steak with onions, peppers, tomatoes and mushrooms on skewers. Baste with dressing or garlic butter while grilling. For garlic butter, mix 3 cloves minced garlic with 6 Tbsps. butter. We serve with rice and, for dipping, we use 1 pkg. original Hidden Valley Ranch Dressing with 1 c. each sour cream and mayonnaise. Serves 4.

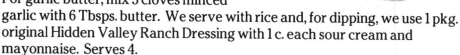

Filet Mignon

Buy tenderloin steaks about 1½ inches thick. Season with salt and pepper. Surround each steak with a lean slice of bacon. Secure with a pick (metal preferred but wood will do). Grill steaks over hot coals approximately 3 minutes per side. Keep a spray bottle of water nearby to douse flames.

Basic Basting Sauce for Fish

2 Tbsps. lemon juice
2 tsps. soy sauce
2 tsps. Worcestershire
2 dashes Tabasco sauce
½ tsp. garlic powder
1 tsp. parsley flakes

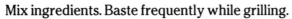

Mix ingredients. Baste frequently while grilling.

Lemon and Herb Marinade for Fish

Especially good for snapper, grouper and dolphin.

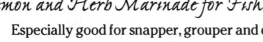

¼ c. olive oil
3 Tbsps. lemon juice
2 cloves garlic, minced
2 bay leaves
¾ tsp. basil
¾ tsp. oregano
2 tsps. dried parsley
Pepper to taste

Simmer 5 to 10 minutes to blend flavors. Remove bay leaves. Cool. Marinate fish for 4 about 30 minutes. Baste with marinade while grilling.

Shrimp Marinade

⅔ c. vegetable oil (part may be olive oil)
3 Tbsps. lemon juice
Few drops Tabasco sauce
1 clove garlic, minced
1 Tbsp. dried parsley
½ tsp. thyme (or, ¼ each: oregano and basil)
Salt and pepper to taste

About 1 c. for up to 2 lbs. shrimp. Marinate shrimp 30 to 60 minutes. Grill 6 to 8 minutes. Careful not to overcook. If desired, serve shrimp on beds of rice with lemon butter. (Lemon butter: 6 to 8 Tbsps. butter with 1 Tbsp. fresh lemon juice.) For a change from rice, serve over pasta dressed lightly with olive oil, butter and tiny slivers of garlic.

Meats

Beef Stroganov

Nice for festive occasions. Before starting to cook the stroganov, everything else should be ready. This dish is ready in about 5 minutes.

1½ lbs. lean tender beef (sirloin, tenderloin)
1 Tbsp. paprika
Salt and freshly ground black pepper
4 Tbsps. unsalted butter or, preferably, clarified butter
1 c. very finely chopped onion
½ c. dry white wine (dry vermouth will do)
1 c. sour cream at room temperature

Cut beef into very thin strips about 3 inches long. Shake in plastic bag with paprika, salt and pepper to coat well. Heat skillet over high heat, melt butter, add beef strips in small batches. Do not overcrowd the pan. Toss and turn while cooking meat to medium-rare, set aside as done. Add onions, stir constantly while browning very briefly, set aside with steak. Add wine, scrape up pan drippings while boiling wine down to just a glaze. Return beef and onions to skillet, reheat briefly, remove from heat, stir in sour cream, serve immediately. Serves 4. Good with buttered rice with minced parsley.

Teriyaki Steak Strips

½ lb. boneless sirloin or flank steak
2 Tbsps. salad oil
2 Tbsps. soy sauce
2 Tbsps. honey
1 Tbsp. vinegar
¾ tsp. powdered ginger
½ tsp. garlic powder

Slice steak diagonally across the grain into ½-inch wide strips 2 to 3 inches long. Marinate 30 minutes or longer in remaining ingredients. Drain, blot dry. Stir-fry in hot oil in skillet or wok, serve over rice. Serves 2.

Creamed Dried Beef

2½-oz. jar dried beef, cut into thin strips
1½ Tbsps. butter
2 Tbsps. plus 1 tsp. flour
1½ c. milk or half-and-half
¾ tsp. Worcestershire sauce
About ½ c. diced peppers, scallions or pimento (optional)

Melt butter in medium saucepan over low heat. Add flour, stir constantly 2 to 3 minutes. Add milk, stir until sauce has thickened. Add more milk if needed. Add remaining ingredients, heat through. Serve over rice, toast, biscuits or noodles. Serves 2.

Easy Beef Stew

1 lb. round steak, ½ to 1-inch cubes
¼ c. flour
½ tsp. paprika
⅛ tsp. pepper
1 Tbsp. each: oil, butter (more as needed)
1 large stalk celery, sliced
1 medium onion, chopped
1 clove garlic, minced
1 large potato, cut into large chunks
14½-oz. can beef broth or
14½-oz. can undrained tomatoes, chopped
2 beef bouillon cubes
1 bay leaf (remove before serving)
Vegetables of choice: *e.g.* corn, peas, beans
Bottled Maggi Seasoning (or salt) to taste

Mix flour, paprika and pepper in plastic bag. Blot meat dry, add to flour mixture, shake to coat completely. Heat a heavy skillet, add oil and butter. Brown beef, a handful at a time. As seared, transfer with a slotted spoon to a heavy saucepan. Add any flour remaining to pot. Rinse skillet. Add a bit more oil and butter. Sauté celery, onion, garlic and potato 5 minutes. Add to pot. Add broth or tomatoes, bouillon cubes and bay leaf. Cover pot tightly, simmer 1 hour or until beef is tender. (May add more broth or tomato sauce, if desired.) Season with Maggi or salt. Add fresh, canned or frozen vegetables of choice. Cook until done. Serves 4.

Italian Meatballs

1½ lbs. good ground beef
1 small onion, minced (optional)
¼ c. minced fresh parsley or 2 Tbsps. dried
¼ c. fine fresh bread crumbs (1 slice)
1 clove garlic, minced
Salt and pepper to taste
¼ c. grated Parmesan

Mix all, shape into about 16 medium-size meatballs. Brown in olive oil, add to tomato sauce, cook through. Serve with pasta and extra Parmesan. Serves 4.

Gourmet Garlic Butter Sauce for Burgers

3 Tbsps. butter
1 Tbsp. chopped garlic
1 Tbsp. chopped shallots
1 Tbsp. chopped parsley
1 tsp. Worcestershire sauce
Salt and pepper to taste

Make sauce in small saucepan. Spoon over pan-broiled beef burgers. Sufficient for 4, or, if spooning extra sauce over rice or noodles, sufficient for 2. *Pierre Franey.* (Chopped green onion or onion may be used in place of shallots.)

Crispy Corned Beef Hash Patties

15½-oz. can corned beef hash
Yellow cornmeal
About 4 Tbsps. butter

Open both ends of the can, push roll of hash out in one piece. Slice into 6 to 8 patties, dip in cornmeal to cover lightly on both sides. Melt butter over medium heat in skillet, fry patties, turning occasionally, until heated through. Serves 2 to 4. *Brig. Gen. Jack Catlin, USAF, Ret.*

VARIATION: Dip patties in seasoned flour, then a beaten egg. Fry until done. Good with corn or lima beans, sliced tomatoes or cole slaw.

Chili Con Carne Wilson

2 Tbsps. salad oil
1½ lbs. good quality ground beef
1 large onion, coarsely chopped
1 medium green pepper, coarsely chopped
2 cloves garlic, minced
28-oz. can tomatoes, with juices, cut up
6-oz. can tomato paste
2 c. water
3 beef bouillon cubes
1½ Tbsps. chili powder or more to taste
1 tsp. each: oregano, paprika, sugar
½ tsp. each: ground cumin, salt
¼ tsp. pepper, salt to taste
15-oz. can kidney beans, drained

Heat oil in large heavy skillet. Brown ground beef in small batches, transfer with slotted spoon to large pot. In skillet, sauté onion, peppers and garlic over medium heat to soften. Transfer to pot. Add remaining except beans, simmer at least 30 minutes. Add beans, heat through. Serves 4 to 6. For a quick chili, I use McCormick Chili Seasoning Mix with its recipe on the package.

Seashells with Sauce Bolognese

2 Tbsps. olive oil
¾ lb. lean ground beef
¼ c. chopped celery
¼ c. chopped carrots
½ c. chopped onion
1 clove garlic, minced
14½-oz. can beef broth or 2 c. bouillon
6-oz. can tomato paste
2 to 4 Tbsps. cream, half-and-half or milk
8 ozs. shell macaroni, cooked
Grated Parmesan or Romano

Heat oil in large skillet, brown beef with vegetables. Drain off excess fat. Add broth and tomato paste. Simmer about 20 minutes allowing sauce to thicken some. Smooth out sauce with cream or milk, spoon over seashell macaroni or other pasta. Top with cheese. Serves 4.

Meatloaf with Tomato Sauce

2 slices bread
¾ c. milk
1 lb. lean ground chuck
Salt and pepper to taste
¼ c. finely chopped celery (optional)
1 small onion, minced (optional)
8-oz. can tomato sauce
1 Tbsp. lemon juice
1 Tbsp. Worcestershire
3 Tbsps. catsup
1 clove garlic, minced
1 to 2 Tbsps. butter
Salt to taste

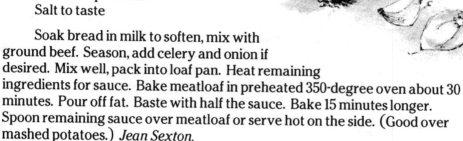

Soak bread in milk to soften, mix with ground beef. Season, add celery and onion if desired. Mix well, pack into loaf pan. Heat remaining ingredients for sauce. Bake meatloaf in preheated 350-degree oven about 30 minutes. Pour off fat. Baste with half the sauce. Bake 15 minutes longer. Spoon remaining sauce over meatloaf or serve hot on the side. (Good over mashed potatoes.) *Jean Sexton.*

Chili Bake

A good "hidden reserve" meal. Bag up the 3 cans and the Fritos and it's almost ready to go.

15-oz. can Hormel chili without beans
15-oz. can Hormel chili with beans
10-oz. can mild enchilada sauce
2 c. coarsely crumbled Fritos
2 (or less) medium onions, finely chopped
2 c. grated Cheddar cheese

Mix chilies and enchilada sauce. Layer in a baking dish (about 7 x 11) half of each: Fritos, chili, onions, cheese. Repeat. Bake in preheated 375-degree oven about 30 minutes. Serves 4 to 6. Some of the onions may be served as a topping. May also offer chopped ripe olives.

Tacos

1 lb. lean ground beef
1 Tbsp. cooking oil
Chili powder, cumin, oregano, paprika, salt, garlic powder
8-oz. can tomato sauce
1 large onion, chopped
2 large tomatoes, diced
1½ c. grated Cheddar
¼ head iceberg lettuce, shredded
Small can ripe olives, drained
Picante sauce
12 corn tortillas
Oil for frying tortillas

Heat oil in a large skillet. Brown the beef, seasoning it with pinches of selected seasonings. Add tomato sauce. Simmer briefly to blend. Meanwhile, fry tortillas one at a time quickly in a small amount of hot oil. Drain on paper towels. Cover with foil to keep warm. (Or, you may use packaged tortilla shells.) Present with toppings to build your own tacos. Serves 4.

Bean and Burger Casserole

1 Tbsp. oil or butter
1 coarsely chopped onion
1 coarsely chopped green pepper
1 lb. lean ground beef
2 16-oz. cans pork and beans
16-oz. can cream-style white (or yellow) corn
1 c. catsup
1 Tbsp. prepared mustard
1 Tbsp. chili powder
2 Tbsps. brown sugar
Salt and pepper to taste
4 slices bacon

Brown ground beef with onions and peppers in oil or butter. Mix remaining ingredients with meat mixture, except bacon. Pour into 9 x 13 or similar baking dish. Lay bacon slices on top Bake uncovered in 350-degree oven until hot, about 50 minutes. Serves 8. *Mary Jane Simerly.*

Spaghetti Pie

8-oz. spaghetti, broken into 2-inch lengths
2 Tbsps. butter
⅓ c. grated Parmesan
½ tsp. salt
¼ tsp. pepper
1 fork-beaten egg
2 Tbsps. olive oil
1½ lbs. lean ground chuck
1 medium onion, chopped
¼ c. chopped green pepper (optional)
2 c. favorite tomato sauce, commercial or homemade
½ tsp. oregano, or to taste
½ tsp. garlic salt , or to taste
1 c. small curd cottage cheese
8 ozs. shredded Mozzarella

Cook spaghetti minimum time suggested. Drain, spoon into baking dish,
9 x 13 or similar. Stir in butter, cheese, seasonings and egg. Combine, spread
evenly in pan. Heat olive oil in skillet. Fry ground beef with onions and peppers
(optional) to brown. Drain off fat. Stir in sauce and seasonings. Spread cottage
cheese over spaghetti. Top with meat mixture. Bake at 350 degrees 30 minutes.
Sprinkle on Mozzarella. Bake 10 minutes longer or until hot throughout.

Quick Tomato Sauce with Ground Beef

2 Tbsps. olive oil
1 lb. lean ground beef
1 large onion, chopped
2 cloves garlic, chopped
28-oz. can tomatoes, drained, chopped, reserve juices
1 tsp. oregano
½ tsp. basil
Salt and pepper to taste

Heat oil in skillet or pot. Add ground beef, onion and garlic. Cook until
meat is browned. Add drained tomatoes and seasonings. Simmer to blend
flavors, thin if needed with juices.

Sausage Pie

½ lb. Jimmy Dean "regular" sausage
1 small onion, finely chopped
3-oz. can sliced or chopped mushrooms, drained
½ c. Ricotta cheese or cottage cheese
2 Tbsps. Parmesan cheese
3 eggs, fork-beaten
½ tsp. salt
½ tsp. oregano
1 refrigerated pie shell (Pillsbury is good)

Brown sausage with onions and mushrooms. Drain. Mix cheeses with eggs and seasonings. Add sausage mixture. Prick pie shell, bake in preheated 375-degree oven about 5 minutes. Fill pie shell with sausage mixture. Bake at 375 degrees about 45 minutes or until knife blade comes out clean when tested with a fork. Serves 6.

Baked Sausage Links

Allow 2 to 4 small link sausages per serving. Place in one layer in a shallow baking pan. Add water to a depth of ¼-inch. Bake, uncovered, in a 400-degree oven 15 minutes. Drain off drippings, return sausages to oven, bake 20 minutes longer. Drain on paper towels. *Chatham County, Ga. Extension Service.*

Baked Beans with Frankfurters

16-oz. can baked beans in tomato sauce
3 or 4 frankfurters
1 medium onion, thinly sliced
¼ c. chili sauce
2 tsps. chili powder
1 c. fine fresh bread crumbs
Parmesan cheese

Pour beans into baking dish. Slice franks into discs. Distribute over beans. Lay thin onion slices over the franks. Mix chili sauce and chili powder, spoon over onions. Sprinkle on the bread crumbs. Cover with a thin layer of Parmesan. Bake at 375 about 30 minutes. Serves 2 or 3. *James Beard, adapted.*

Sausage Strata

8 slices firm white bread (e.g. Pepperidge Farm), divided
¾ lb. Monterey Jack cheese, grated, divided
½ lb. bulk sausage (I like Jimmy Dean "Medium")
4 large eggs, beaten lightly
½ tsp. salt
½ tsp. Worcestershire sauce
1 tsp. Dijon mustard
Pinch cayenne
3 Tbsps. melted butter, cooled

Butter an 8 x 8 (or similar) baking pan. Brown sausage, drain, set aside. Remove crusts from bread, cut into ½-inch cubes. Distribute one-third of the bread cubes over bottom of baking dish. Add one-third amount of cheese. Add all the sausage. Add half the bread remaining, then half the cheese remaining, then all the remaining bread crumbs. Whisk together the eggs, milk and seasonings. Slowly pour over casserole ingredients. Top with remaining cheese and the butter. Cover. Chill at least an hour or overnight. Bake in 350 degree oven about 50 minutes or until browned. Serves 4.

Hot Potatoes and Sausage

3 slices bacon, diced
8-oz. kielbasa, 4-in. lengths, halved lengthwise
1 Tbsp. butter or olive oil
1 or 2 cloves garlic, minced
4 or more green onions, chopped
2 large potatoes, parboiled, sliced,
  or 2 uncooked potatoes, diced
Pinch each: thyme, crushed red pepper
2 Tbsps. red wine vinegar
Salt and freshly-ground black pepper to taste
2 Tbsps. fresh chopped parsley (optional)

Sauté bacon in a large skillet until soft but not browned. Set aside with slotted spoon. Brown sausage pieces in the bacon fat. Set aside with bacon. Discard fat. Heat butter or oil, add garlic, green onions, potatoes, thyme and red pepper. Stirring frequently, cook until potatoes are done, 15 to 20 minutes. Return bacon and sausage to pan, add vinegar, salt and pepper. Serves 2 to 3. A one-skillet favorite.

Lentils with Polish Sausage

Smoky, nutty, nourishing.

4 Tbsps. butter or 2 Tbsps. each butter, oil
1½ c. chopped onion
1 clove garlic, minced
1½ Tbsps. sweet Hungarian paprika
1 lb. Polish sausage, ¼-in. slices
1 c. uncooked lentils
½ tsp. marjoram
Salt and pepper to taste
3 c. water
2 Tbsps. minced parsley

Melt fat in a large skillet. Sauté onions and garlic until soft. Add paprika and sausage, sauté until sausage is browned. Discard excess fat. Transfer to saucepan if desired. Add lentils, marjoram, salt, pepper and water. Bring mixture to a boil. Lower heat, and, stirring occasionally, simmer uncovered about 45 minutes or until lentils are tender. Sprinkle with parsley. Serves 4. Good with salad and bread.

Fettuccine and Sausage

8 ozs. fettuccine
8 to 12 ozs. smoked sausage, thinly sliced (coins)
2 Tbsps. olive oil
1 onion, chopped
1 clove garlic, minced
½ green pepper, diced
½ red pepper, diced
¼ c. chopped fresh parsley
Parmesan, grated

While fettuccine cooks, brown sausage in large skillet. Set aside when browned. Heat olive oil in skillet. Stir-fry vegetables, except parsley, over medium heat until crisp-tender. Return sausage to skillet. Heat through, stir in parsley. If desired, add a little olive oil to cooked pasta to moisten, then top with sausage mixture. Pass the Parmesan. Serves 2.

$\mathcal{P}$ork chops are very versatile. Look for well-cut, well-trimmed chops, with bones or boneless. We like to freeze pork chops and other meats in small flat packages which fit well in our small boat freezer.

Usually a recipe for pork chops calls for browning the meat before proceeding with the recipe. This is best done in a very hot skillet, and, if butter is used, it is likely to burn. While butter will burn less quickly if it is mixed with oil, we find it worthwhile to have on hand some CLARIFIED BUTTER, not only for browning meats, but for grilling sandwiches, frying eggs, sautéing onions and the like.

To clarify (remove salt from) butter, cut up a stick or more of butter and put in a small saucepan or skillet. Melt slowly, remove from heat, rest a few minutes, then pour the clear liquid into a small bowl or cup. The salty portion may be used for vegetables.

Pork Chop Sauté with Peppers

4 medium rib or loin pork chops,
   fat removed
Salt, pepper, paprika, thyme
1 Tbsp. vegetable or olive oil
1 Tbsp. butter
1 green pepper, thinly sliced ⎫
1 red pepper, thinly-sliced ⎬ (may use 2 green peppers)
1 medium onion, thinly-sliced ⎭
1 or 2 cloves garlic, minced
¼ c. water, wine, broth or bouillon (add more if needed)

Season chops with salt, pepper, paprika and thyme, rubbing in seasonings. Set aside. Heat oil and butter in large skillet over medium heat. Stirring, quickly sauté peppers, onion and garlic about 5 minutes. Set vegetables aside. Brown chops, both sides. Reduce heat, cover skillet, cook over low heat until chops are tender — 45 tp 60 minutes. (May wish to use heat diffuser on burner.) Uncover, top with the vegetables, cook until vegetables are heated through. May wish to thicken pan juices. Mix about 2 tsps. softened butter wth 2 tsps. flour. Add by bits to simmering pan juices. Stir constantly until juices are of desired consistency.

Orange Glazed Pork Chops

4 pork chops, ¾-inch thick, trimmed of fat
Salt and pepper to taste
1 Tbsp. vegetable oil
½ c. orange juice
2 Tbsps. each: brown sugar, orange marmalade
1 Tbsp. vinegar

Season chops with salt and pepper. Heat oil in large skillet. Brown chops on both sides. Discard excess fat. Combine remaining ingredients, pour over chops. Cover skillet, simmer 45 minutes or until chops are tender. Nice with rice. Serves 4.

Pork Medallions with Glazed Apples

¾ lb. thin boneless pork chops or slices of pork tenderloin
½ c. flour
Salt, pepper, garlic powder, paprika
Clarified or unsalted butter, or a little oil and butter mixed
1 large unpeeled tart apple, cored, sliced
Brown sugar

Mix seasonings with flour. Dredge slices of pork in flour mixed with seasonings. Shake off excess. Heat butter or oil and butter in a large skillet. Turning frequently, cook chops until crisp, brown and tender, 8 to 10 minutes. If needed, add a little water to keep chops from sticking. Set aside when done, cover with foil to keep warm. Add a little butter to the skillet. Add apple slices, turn frequently while browning on both sides. Sprinkle with brown sugar. When melted and glazed, serve apples with pork. Serves 2.

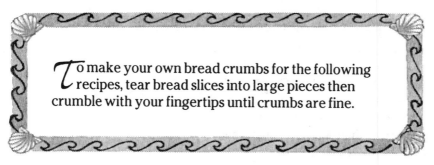

To make your own bread crumbs for the following recipes, tear bread slices into large pieces then crumble with your fingertips until crumbs are fine.

Breaded Pork Cutlets (Schnitzels)

4 thin boneless pork chops
About 3 Tbsps. flour
Salt and pepper to taste
1 egg fork-beaten with 1 Tbsp. water
1 c. (or more) fine fresh bread crumbs
¼ c. grated Parmesan cheese
2 Tbsps. each: vegetable or olive oil, butter
Lemon wedges

Dredge chops lightly in seasoned flour. Dip in egg, coat well with crumbs mixed with Parmesan. Heat oil and butter in large skillet, brown cutlets, reduce heat. Turning occasionally, cook about 8 minutes on each side over low heat. Serve with lemon wedges. Serves 2 to 4. (Foil pie plates are handy for the egg wash and the crumbs.)

Breaded Pork Cutlets a la Parmigiana

Prepare cutlets as described above. Spoon about 2 Tbsps. (meatless) spaghetti sauce over each hot cooked cutlet. Top with a slice of Mozzarella cheese or grated Mozzarella. Sprinkle with Parmesan. Broil in middle of oven until the cheese melts. (Delicious with cooked noodles dressed with a bit of butter and olive oil, tiny slivers of garlic and chopped parsley. Serve with extra tomato sauce if you wish.)

Breaded Pork Cutlets with Ham and Swiss Cheese

Prepare cutlets as above. Preheat oven to 400 degrees. Place cutlets in a baking dish. Top each hot cutlet with a thin slice of ham or prosciutto. Add a thin slice of Swiss cheese. Bake uncovered until cheese melts.

Pork Chops Baked with Rice

    4 medium pork chops, rib, loin or boneless
    Salt, pepper, thyme or sage, paprika
    1 Tbsp. each: unsalted butter, oil or all oil
    1½ c. uncooked rice
    3 c. chicken, beef or vegetable broth (or bouillon)
    1 each: green pepper, large onion, sliced
    2 firm tomatoes, sliced

Sprinkle chops with seasonings. Brown in a skillet in oil or butter. Spread rice over bottom of greased baking dish, about 7 x 11. Pour broth over rice. Lay pepper, onion and tomato slices evenly over chops. Cover tightly with 2 layers of foil. Bake in preheated 350-degree oven about 1 hour, or until rice has absorbed broth and chops are tender.

Pork Chops with Sweet and Sour Sauce

    4 pork chops, trimmed of excess fat
    Salt, pepper, paprika
    1 Tbsp. vegetable oil
    1 large onion, sliced
    8-oz. can tomato sauce
    ⅓ c. brown sugar
    ¼ c. vinegar
    1 Tbsp. Worcestershire sauce

Season chops with salt, pepper and paprika. Brown in large skillet in hot oil. Add onion, stir to brown and soften. Add remaining ingredients, cover, cook on low heat until chops are tender, 30 to 40 minutes.

Notes / Extra Recipe

Ham in Curry Sauce

2 Tbsps. butter
¼ tsp. curry powder, or more to taste
2 Tbsps. flour
1¼ c. milk (may use some half-and-half)
Salt and pepper to taste
¼ to ½ c. diced red and/or green peppers or ¼ c. diced pimentos
½ c. diced ham

Melt butter in medium saucepan over medium heat. Add curry powder, stir and cook 1 minute. Add flour, and, stirring constantly, cook about 2 minutes. Add milk gradually, stir constantly until thickened. Add seasonings, ham and peppers or pimentos. Simmer about 10 minutes. Present in patty shells, over rice or noodles. Serves 2.

Pan Broiled Ham Steaks

Fully-cooked ham steak, ½ to ¾ lb.
1 Tbsp. butter
1 Tbsp. Dijon mustard
1 Tbsp. honey

Mix mustard and honey. Melt butter in medium skillet. Fry ham over moderate heat 8 to 10 minutes. Turn frequently, basting lightly with honey-mustard. Reserve most of sauce to spread on at end. Serves 2.

VARIATION: Use a can of 4 pineapple slices. Mix a few tablespoons pineapple juice with honey-mustard. Also, use some of the juice for basting ham while cooking. At end, set ham aside, keep warm, and brown pineapple slices lightly in skillet.

Ham Steak with Pineapple Sauce

¼ c. pineapple preserves
1 Tbsp. Dijon mustard
1 tsp. Worcestershire sauce
Pinch of powdered cloves (optional)
2 Tbsps. butter
Ham steak, ½ to ¾ lb.

Make sauce of preserves, mustard, Worcestershire and, if desired, cloves. Heat butter in medium skillet, fry ham about 10 minutes, basting frequently with sauce. Reserve most of the sauce for the end. Canned pineapple slices may be heated briefly in the syrupy sauce. Add a little juice if needed. Serves 2.

Raisin Sauce for Ham

¼ c. orange juice or pineapple juice
¼ c. water (or use all juice or all water)
2 Tbsps. white or cider vinegar
¼ c. brown sugar
¼ tsp. dry mustard
½ Tbsp. flour
1 Tbsp. butter
2 to 4 Tbsps. raisins

Mix ingredients in a small saucepan. Cook slowly until syrupy. While sauce is cooking, if you wish, spoon or brush some of the sauce on a ham steak which is being pan-fried, oven-baked or broiled. Spoon sauce over ham when serving. Sufficient sauce for 2 to 4.

Fettuccine with Ham and Tomatoes

All the ingredients should be ready before cooking starts.

9-oz. pkg. fresh fettuccine (or use dried)
6 Tbsps. butter
1 bunch green onions, tops removed, chopped
2 cloves garlic, minced
1 c. cherry tomatoes, halved, or diced plum tomatoes
1 c. ham slices, about 3" long by ½" wide
1 egg yolk
¼ c. heavy cream
½ c. freshly grated Parmesan
Salt and ground pepper to taste

While pasta cooks to "al dente" stage, melt butter in a large skillet. (When pasta is done, drain, cover to keep warm.) Add green onions and garlic to skillet, stirring, cook a few minutes. Add tomatoes and ham. Stir until hot. Beat egg yolk in a small bowl. Add cream, stir just until well-mixed. Off heat, add cream mixture to ham mixture. Return to low heat, (do not boil), stir to blend and heat through. Remove from heat, add Parmesan, season, serve immediately over hot pasta. Serves 4. *Jr. League, Palo Alto, adapted.*

Veal alla Francese

Thin slices of veal cook very quickly, so the rest of the meal must be ready.

4 scallops of veal, ¼ to ½ lb. total
Salt, freshly-ground pepper, flour
1 egg whipped with 1 Tbsp. water
1 Tbsp. each: olive oil, unsalted butter
About 1 additional Tbsp. butter
1 to 2 Tbsps. fresh lemon juice
Lemon wedges

Season veal with salt and pepper, sprinkle with flour to coat each side thoroughly. Dip veal in the beaten egg, allow excess to run off. In a large skillet, heat olive oil and butter over moderately high heat until hot. Cook veal 2 to 3 minutes on each side, turning a time or two. Do not overcrowd skillet. Cook the veal scallops in 2 or 3 batches. As they are done, set them aside on a plate covered with foil. Add the additional butter and the lemon juice to skillet, scrape up drippings, spoon over veal. Serve immediately with lemon wedges. Serves 2.

Veal Scallopini

⅓ to ½ lb. thin scallops of veal
Flour, salt, pepper
1 fork-beaten egg
2 or 3 slices bread, crumbled for fine crumbs
2 Tbsps. grated Parmesan (optional)
1 Tbsp. each: olive oil, butter (more if needed)
Lemon wedges

Gently pound veal between sheets of wax paper to ¼-inch thickness. Coat with seasoned flour. Dip in egg, then in crumbs mixed with Parmesan if desired. Cover completely with crumbs, pressing on firmly. (May prepare ahead.) Heat oil and butter in large skillet, sauté veal quickly over moderate heat until golden brown, 2 to 3 minutes each side. Garnish with lemon wedges. Serves 2.

Pan Broiled Lamb Chops

Before pan-broiling lamb chops, we like to marinate in the following mixture for at least an hour.

¼ c. salad oil
2 Tbsps. fresh lemon juice
½ tsp. salt
⅛ tsp. pepper
1 clove garlic, minced

Remove the chops from the marinade, blot dry. Brown over moderately high heat in unsalted butter, or a little butter mixed with a little oil. Reduce heat, turn frequently, cook over low heat until done, an average of 10 minutes for medium-thick chops.

Oven Broiled Lamb Chops

4 loin lamb chops, about 1½ inches
Salt and freshly ground black pepper
Mint jelly or mint sauce

Preheat broiler. Season chops, place on rack of broiler pan. Set chops about 5 inches from heat source in oven. Broil 5 minutes, turn, broil second side until nicely browned, about 5 minutes. Garnish with mint jelly or sauce. Serves 4.

Lemon and Caper Sauce for Lamb Chops

2 Tbsps. each: butter, lemon juice
Dash Worcestershire sauce
2 tsps. drained capers
2 Tbsps. fresh chopped parsley, preferred, or 1 tsp. dried parsley
Salt and pepper to taste

Simmer ingredients in a small saucepan. Spoon over broiled chops. Serves 4.

Notes / Extra Recipe

Vegetables, Rice & Noodles

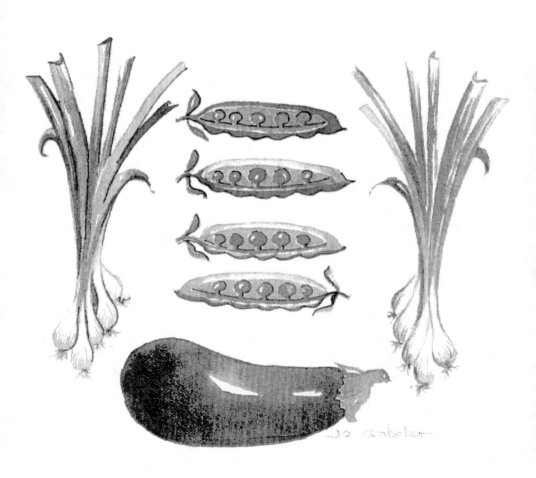

Vegetables

*O*ne of my favorite cookbooks is all about vegetables. It is *The Victory Garden Cookbook* by Marian Morash. I recommend it highly for cruisers who love vegetables. While there are hundreds of wonderful ways to present vegetables, for galley cooking, especially, we favor simplicity. The first recipe, however, is not for a vegetable but for apples which are a good substitute for a vegetable with ham or pork.

Sautéed Apple Rings

Core firm unpeeled apples (green Granny Smiths are good). Cut into ½ to ¾-inch thick slices. For each apple, melt about 2 Tbsps. butter over medium heat in a large skillet. Add apple slices, sprinkle lightly with granulated sugar. Sauté 2 to 3 minutes, sprinkle again with sugar. Cook until browned but still firm, about 5 minutes.

Asparagus

Allow ⅓ to ½ lb. per person. Snap off tough ends. Unless asparagus are young and tender, scrape the lower portions with a vegetable peeler or paring knife. In a large skillet, bring to a boil enough salted water to just cover the asparagus. Add asparagus to the boiling water, cook uncovered 3 to 5 minutes. Drain. Delightful with butter and lemon juice or lemon juice alone.

Stir-Fry Asparagus

Rinse asparagus, pat dry. Snap off tough ends, cut stalks at a 45-degree angle into 2-inch pieces. Heat enough oil in a skillet to just cover the bottom of the pan. When the oil is hot, add the asparagus pieces, stir-fry 3 to 5 minutes over medium heat. When half done, season with garlic salt or add a little soy sauce and/or sesame seed oil. *Ellen Lew.*

Steamed Broccoli

Place a collapsible vegetable steamer in a saucepan with about 1 inch of boiling water. Separate florets. Stems may be used, too, but must be peeled with a knife or vegetable parer. Cut them into small pieces. Place florets and stems into steamer, cover, cook 3 to 4 minutes until just tender. Season with butter or olive oil, salt and pepper and lemon juice if desired.

Blanched Broccoli

For 4, use about 1½ lbs. fresh broccoli. Separate florets, peel and slice stems if desired. Bring to a boil enough salted water to cover broccoli. Add broccoli, cook uncovered 4 to 5 minutes, drain. Heat a few tablespoons butter in the saucepan, return broccoli to pan, sprinkle with salt and pepper, stir to mix. Add some lemon juice if desired.

Blanched Brussels Sprouts

Allow about 6 small brussels sprouts per person. Slice off bottoms of stems, pull off withered leaves. For quick cooking, cut an x in stem end. Bring to a boil lightly salted water to cover sprouts. Cook sprouts about 5 minutes. Drain, rinse with cold water, return to saucepan. Stir in butter, salt and pepper. (Shallots mix well with brussels sprouts. May sauté some shallots in butter in saucepan before returning sprouts to the pan.)

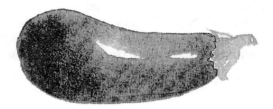

Fresh Green Beans

Rinse beans, snip off ends. Bring to a boil sufficient salted water to cover beans. Drop beans into boiling water, return water to a boil, cook beans about 5 minutes. Drain. Melt some butter in the pan, reheat beans in butter, season with salt and pepper.

Green Beans Amandine

Cook green beans as above. Melt ¼ c. butter. Sauté in butter until lightly browned ¼ c. slivered almonds. Add salt.

Pasta E Fagioli (pasta and beans)

A potful of goodness from easily stored staples.

¼ c. (measured dry) elbow macaroni
2 Tbsps. olive oil
1 small onion, coarsely chopped
1 large clove garlic, minced
1 Tbsp. dried parsley
½ tsp. oregano
Pinch crushed red pepper flakes
28-oz. can tomatoes, Italian preferred, chopped
Salt and pepper to taste
15-oz. can kidney beans or cannelloni, undrained
Parmesan cheese

Cook macaroni, drain, set aside. Heat olive oil in medium pot, sauté onion and garlic with parsley, oregano and red pepper flakes about 5 minutes. Add tomatoes, season with salt and pepper, simmer 20 to 30 minutes. Add macaroni and beans, heat through. If necessary, thin with a little water. Serve in soup bowls, sprinkle with Parmesan. Makes 1 quart, serves 3 or 4. Add leftovers to beef or chicken broth for soup.

Baked Beans

4 slices bacon, cooked until crisp, crumbled
19-oz. can baked beans
1 medium onion, thinly sliced
3 Tbsps. catsup
3 Tbsps. brown sugar
1 Tbsp. vinegar
¼ tsp. dry mustard

Mix and bake about 45 minutes at 350 degrees. Serves 2 to 3.

Sitr-Fry Cabbage with Celery

Slice cabbage thinly. Cut celery on the diagonal into thin pieces. Stir-fry in a skillet in a little hot peanut or vegetable oil 3 to 5 minutes. Season with salt and pepper and a splash of vinegar or soy sauce.

Carrots and Peppers

    2 tsps. each: olive oil, butter
    4 carrots, cut into matchsticks
    1 red pepper, thin strips
    Salt and pepper
    Chopped parsley

Heat oil and butter in a large skillet. Stir-fry vegetables over medium heat about 5 minutes. Top with chopped parsley for additional color. Serves 3 to 4.

Glazed Carrots

    1 lb. carrots, cut into thin rounds or strips
    Salt and pepper
    Water or orange juice or a mixture
    2 Tbsps. butter
    1½ tsps. sugar
    Chopped parsley (optional)

Place carrots in a saucepan or skillet. Season with salt and pepper. Barely cover with water or juice or the mixture. Add butter and sugar. Cover. Bring to a boil. Boil gently about 10 minutes. Uncover, continue cooking until liquid has evaporated leaving carrots lightly browned and glazed. If desired, sprinkle with parsley. Serves 4.

Carrots Julienne with Rosemary

    1 Tbsp. butter
    1 Tbsp. finely chopped onion
    2 large carrots, scraped, cut into thin strips
    ⅓ c. orange juice
    ⅓ tsp. dried rosemary, crushed
    1 Tbsp. fresh chopped parsley or 1 tsp. dried
    Salt and pepper to taste

Melt butter in a small skillet. Add onion, sauté to soften. Add carrot strips, orange juice and rosemary. Boil gently until carrots are tender, 5 to 10 minutes. Stir in parsley, season with salt and pepper. Serves 2.

Cauliflower

A 1½ lb. head of cauliflower will serve 4. Drop florets into a pot of salted boiling water, cook, uncovered, 5 to 8 minutes. Drain. Drizzle with melted butter. If desired, sprinkle with Parmesan and a little paprika.

Cauliflower in Cheese Sauce

Cook 1 head cauliflower as above. Make a white sauce of 2 Tbsps. each butter and flour, 1¼ c. milk and ½ c. grated cheddar or Swiss (or other) cheese. Season with salt, pepper and cayenne to taste. Add cooked cauliflower to sauce. Heat through. (Sauce is good for broccoli, too.)

Red Beans and Rice

Flavorful, rib-sticking', delicious New Orleans soul food. Make at home and freeze in serving- sized packets.

12-oz. pkg. dried red beans
3 qts. water
2 or 3 ham hocks (or large ham bone)
2 large celery stalks, chopped
1 each, chopped: large onion, green pepper
3 garlic cloves, minced
6 strips bacon, drippings reserved
8-oz. smoked sausage, thinly sliced, slices halved
¼ lb. ham, diced (I use a ham steak)
2 bay leaves (remove when serving)
Small pinch each: oregano, cumin, pepper, chili powder

Rinse beans, soak in a large pot, covered with water, overnight or several hours. Drain, rinse, return beans to pot. Add the 3 quarts water and ham hocks and/or bone. Start cooking, uncovered, over low heat. (I place pot on a heat deflector.) Meanwhile, cook bacon until nearly done, but not crispy. In bacon drippings, sauté vegetables until softened. After skimming froth from top of beans, add vegetables to pot. Sauté sausage and ham. Drain. Add to pot with bacon, cut up. Cook, partially covered, over low heat, stirring occasionally, until beans are soft and creamy, about 2½ hours. If too thick, add water, or, too thin, boil to reduce liquid. Cool, refrigerate, spoon off or blot off with paper towel any congealed fat. Serve over mounds of hot fluffy rice. Serves 8. *Jo Gabeler Brooks, adapted.*

Sautéed Mushrooms

Slice or quarter 1 lb. cleaned fresh mushrooms to serve 4. Sprinkle with 1 Tbsp. fresh lemon juice. Stirring, sauté mushrooms and 1 tsp. minced garlic in 2 Tbsp. each olive oil and butter. Cook until mushrooms absorb the oil and butter. Season with salt and pepper and additional lemon juice. Top with chopped parsley if you wish.

Peas and Mushrooms with Cream

Thaw, but do not cook, 1 pkg frozen peas. Drain, pat dry. Heat 1 Tbsp. butter in a skillet or saucepan. Briefly sauté 1 clove minced garlic and 4 coarsely chopped green onions. Add 8 ozs. fresh mushrooms, sliced. Sauté 3 minutes. Add peas, season with salt and pepper. Add ½ c. heavy cream. Stirring, boil gently until cream is reduced and thickened. Delicious when you need a "moist" vegetable dish. Serves 4.

Sautéed Onions

Slice onions thinly, sauté to a deep golden brown in a little oil and butter. Season with salt and pepper. Irresistible with pan-broiled steak or burgers.

Potato Wafers

Peel and cut 2 large potatoes into ¼-inch slices. Heat about 2 Tbsps. oil and 1 Tbsp. butter in a skillet. Turning often, cook potatoes until browned and tender, about 15 minutes. May cook a sliced onion with potatoes. Season with salt and pepper. Serves 2.

Sautéed New Potatoes

Boil small, thin-skinned, unpeeled red or white potatoes about 10 minutes, until cooked but still firm. Do not peel. Refrigerate until cooking time. Dice potatoes. Fry in a little oil and butter until done. Chopped onion, chopped red and/or green pepper, and minced garlic may be added while cooking. Season with salt and pepper.

Mashed Potatoes AuGratin

Mash potatoes as usual with milk and butter, salt and pepper. Spoon into a baking dish. Cover with lots of grated cheese. Bake at 375 about 20 minutes.

Rosti

Delicious Swiss-style potatoes. Boil unpeeled, plain white potatoes until just tender. Cool, refrigerate. Before cooking, peel, shred on a coarse grater or with food processor. Season with salt and pepper. In a large skillet, melt 1 Tbsp. butter for each potato. Let the butter bubble, add potatoes to pan, stir until coated with butter. Mound in center of skillet. Add 1 Tbsp. hot water for each 2 potatoes. Cover and cook about 15 minutes. Serve as is or flip onto serving platter. *Marilyn Newman.*

Spinach Casserole

2 pkgs. frozen chopped spinach, well-drained,
3-oz. pkg. cream cheese, softened
4 Tbsps. butter, softened
1 c. Pepperidge Farm herb dressing
4 Tbsps. melted butter

Mix cream cheese with softened butter. Stir into spinach. Place in baking dish. Mix dressing with the melted butter. Cover spinach. Bake at 350 degrees about 30 minutes. Serves 4 to 5.

Baked Spinach with Mushrooms

2 pkgs. frozen chopped spinach, well-drained
2 Tbsps. butter
¼ lb. fresh mushrooms, sliced
2 cloves garlic, minced
¼ c. cream or milk
¼ c. grated Parmesan

Place spinach in a baking dish. Heat butter in a small skillet. Stirring, sauté mushrooms and garlic until mushroom juices evaporate. Add mushrooms to spinach. Season with salt and pepper. Add cream or milk. Sprinkle with cheese. Bake at 350 degrees about 30 minutes. Serves 4 to 6.

Snow Peas with Garlic

Snip ends off 1 lb. snow peas. Heat 2 Tbsps. vegetable or peanut oil in a large skillet. Add snow peas and 2 cloves garlic, minced. Season with salt and pepper. Stirring, cook over moderate heat 3 to 5 minutes. Serves 3 to 4.

VARIATION: Add ½ c. thinly sliced water chestnuts for each 1 lb. snow peas. Add a little powdered ginger, or minced ginger root, and a bit of soy sauce.

Steamed Snow Peas

Snip ends off snow peas. Place in vegetable steamer set over about an inch of boiling water. Cover, steam about 3 minutes. Season with salt, pepper and butter.

Sautéed Yellow Squash

Trim ends from squash, peel if you wish, slice thinly. Sprinkle with salt. If possible, let drain about 30 minutes to draw out excess water. Blot dry. In a skillet, heat about 2 Tbsps. butter. Sauté 1 small onion, chopped, and 1 clove of garlic, minced. Add squash, stir and cook 3 to 5 minutes.

VARIATION: Add a generous pinch of brown sugar to sautéed squash, stir to mix.

Lemon Squash

Wash ¼ lb. yellow squash or zucchini or a mixture. Slice into ¼-inch slices. Set in steamer basket over boiling water. Steam, covered, until tender, 2 to 3 minutes. Dress with juice of half a lemon, about a tablespoon of olive oil, freshly-ground pepper and salt if needed. Serves 2 generously.

Baked Tomatoes

4 medium to large tomatoes
½ c. bread crumbs
¼ c. Parmesan cheese
½ tsp. garlic salt or to taste
¼ tsp. pepper
6 Tbsps. melted butter or
3 Tbsps. each: melted butter, olive oil

Cut tomatoes in half crosswise. Remove some pulp if desired. Place tomatoes in greased baking pan. Combine ingredients remaining. Spoon mixture on tomatoes. Bring to room temperature if refrigerated. Bake uncovered in 350-degree oven 20 minutes or less time in a hotter oven. Serves 4.

Broiled Tomatoes

Preheat broiler. Slice tomatoes in half crosswise. Place in oiled baking pan. Sprinkle with finely minced garlic, crumbled oregano, salt and coarse-ground black pepper. Drizzle each half with 1 to 2 tsps. olive oil. Broil about 5 inches from heat source 3 to 5 minutes.

Fried Tomatoes

Cut each firm, ripe tomato into 3 or 4 thick slices. In a shallow bowl, mix a little flour seasoned with salt, or garlic salt, and pepper. Dredge tomato slices in flour to coat lightly on both sides. Heat enough olive oil, or butter and olive oil, to glaze the bottom of a skillet. When moderately hot, fry tomatoes over medium heat 1 to 2 minutes per side.

Zucchini Sauté

Rinse, and, if desired, peel small or medium zucchini. Cut into thin strips or small cubes. Heat about 2 Tbsps. olive oil in a skillet until quite hot. Keep the skillet hot, add zucchini, sprinkle with garlic salt, stir-fry quickly about 3 minutes. Do not overcook. If you wish, sprinkle with Parmesan.

Tomatoes Topped with Spinach

1 box frozen spinach, cooked
1 medium onion, minced
1 Tbsp. butter
Salt and pepper
Parmesan cheese

Sauté onion in butter. Add to spinach. Season with salt and pepper. Spoon mounds on tops of thick-sliced tomatoes. Sprinkle with Parmesan. Bake in 400-degree oven about 10 minutes.

Quick Baked Zucchini

For 2, peel 2 to 3 medium zucchini. Dice into ¼-inch cubes. Mix 1 Tbsp. olive oil with 1 or 2 cloves of garlic, minced. Place zucchini in one layer in a baking pan. Sprinkle with salt and freshly-ground black pepper. Add the olive oil, mix well. Bake in preheated 450-degree oven about 8 minutes. Do not overcook. Zucchini should be crunchy.

Zucchini and Carrots

¾ lb. each: zucchini, carrots
Salt and pepper
6 Tbsps. butter or 3 Tbsps. each: olive oil, butter

Slice unpeeled zucchini and scraped carrots into ¼-inch julienne slices. Place vegetable steamer in a saucepan with about 1 inch of boiling water. Place carrots in steamer basket, zucchini over carrots. Partially cover pan, steam until vegetables are crisp-tender, about 8 minutes. Season with salt and pepper and coat with butter or olive oil and butter. Serves 6.

Vegetable Medley with Pasta

May substitute other vegetables.

2 Tbsps. olive oil
½ small onion, sliced
1 clove garlic, minced
½ red pepper, sliced
½ green pepper, sliced
1 small zucchini, peeled, cut into strips
About 8 large mushrooms, sliced
Salt and pepper to taste
Few pinches of basil
¼ c. cream (heavy cream preferred)
8 ozs. linguini, or other pasta, cooked
Parmesan cheese

Heat olive oil over moderately high heat in a large skillet. Stir-fry vegetables about 5 minutes. Season to taste. Stir in cream. Serve over pasta, sprinkle with Parmesan. Serves 2 to 3

Spinach Lasagna

10-oz. pkg. frozen chopped spinach, cooked
1 Tbsp. fresh chopped parsley or 1 tsp. dried
1 clove garlic, minced
1 lb. small curd cottage cheese
1 egg
2 Tbsps. butter, softened
½ tsp. salt
⅛ tsp. pepper
Pinch nutmeg
4 ozs. lasagna noodles, cooked
8 ozs. Monterey Jack cheese, shredded
½ c. grated Parmesan cheese
2 c. spaghetti sauce

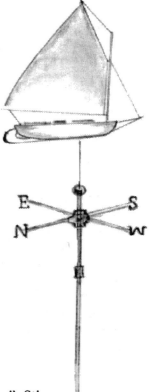

Mix well-drained spinach with parsley, garlic, cottage cheese, egg, butter and seasonings. In a baking dish, 8 x 8 or similar, layer 1/3 the noodles (cut into thinner, shorter strips), the spinach mixture, 1/3 the cheeses. Repeat. Place remaining noodles and cheese on top Bake uncovered 30 minutes or until hot throughout. Serve with sauce on side. Serves 4.

Boiled Rice

1 c. long-grain rice
2 c. water or broth
1 tsp. salt
1 to 2 Tbsps. butter, salad oil or olive oil

Put ingredients into a saucepan. Bring to a boil. Stir thoroughly one time, cover, simmer 15 minutes. About 2 cups to serve 4. If too much liquid is left, uncover, set over low heat a few minutes. If not tender, but liquid has boiled away, sprinkle on droplets of water, cover, cook a few minutes longer.

Rice with Pasta

Cook as Boiled Rice but substitute ¼ c. broken-up spaghetti, vermicelli or linguini for ¼ c. of the rice. That is, use ¾ c. rice, ¼ c. pasta. To vary, brown the rice and pasta in a little oil or butter with a small minced onion. Add 2 c. boiling water or broth and cook, covered, about 15 minutes.

Parmesan Rice

Toss 2 c. cooked rice with a little butter and ½ c. grated Parmesan. Serves 4.. Good with fish.

Herbed Rice

Toss 2 c. cooked rice with 2 Tbsps. chopped parsley and 1 Tbsp. chopped chives. May also add a pinch of dried chervil or tarragon.

Red and Green Rice

Mix ¼ c. chopped pimento with a little olive oil. Mix with 2 c. cooked rice. Garnish rice with 1 Tbsp. chopped parsley.

Rice with Almonds

Toast ⅓ c. sliced almonds in 2 Tbsps. butter. Toss with 2 c. cooked rice.

Rice and Peas

Mix 2 c. cooked rice and 2 c. buttered cooked peas. Add a pinch of dried tarragon, 1 tsp. dried parsley, salt and pepper. May sprinkle with Parmesan. Good with chicken and veal.

Rice Pilaf

2 Tbsps. butter
¼ c. minced onion
1 c. rice
Salt and pepper to taste
14½-oz. can chicken broth or 2 c. homemade
Fresh chopped parsley, optional

Heat butter in medium saucepan. Add onion, stir frequently until softened. Add rice, stir and cook until golden. Season with salt and pepper, cover with broth, cook, covered, 15 minutes or until done. Serves 4.

Rice with Raisins and Almonds

2 Tbsps. butter
¼ c. finely chopped onion
1 c. rice
2 Tbsps. raisins
¼ c. slivered almonds
2 c. chicken broth or bouillon

Melt butter in medium saucepan. Add onion, cook and stir until softened. Add rice, raisins, almonds and broth or bouillon. Stir to mix, season with salt and pepper, cover, bring to a boil. Reduce heat, cook, covered, 15 minutes or until done. Serves 4.

Rice with Curry Seasoning

2 Tbsps. butter
1 small onion, finely chopped
1 tsp. curry powder
1 c. rice
2 c. chicken broth or bouillon

Heat butter in saucepan. Cook onion until soft and golden. Stir in curry powder, cook and stir about 1 minute to release curry flavor. Add rice and broth or bouillon. Cover, cook about 15 minutes or until done. Serves 4.

Baked Rice

Put 1 c. rice into baking dish. Add 1 tsp. salt, (less if using bouillon), and 1 to 2 Tbsps. butter. Cover with 2 c. boiling broth, water or bouillon. Bake, covered, in preheated 350-degree oven about 30 minutes. (If the liquid is cold instead of boiling when added to rice, cooking time will nearly double.) Serves 4.

VARIATION: Stud a whole peeled onion with 8 whole cloves. Place in baking dish with rice. Add liquid. Cover, bake rice, remove onion.

Lentils and Rice

3 Tbsps. olive oil
1 medium onion, finely chopped
½ c. dried lentils
2½ c. water
1 tsp. salt
½ c. uncooked rice
Chopped fresh parsley, optional

Sauté onions in olive oil in medium saucepan. When soft, add remaining ingredients. Simmer covered until lentils and rice are cooked and liquid is absorbed, about 30 minutes. Sprinkle with parsley if desired. Serves 4.

Black Beans and Rice

2 Tbsps. olive oil
1 c. chopped onion
1 c. chopped green pepper
14½-oz. can undrained tomatoes, chopped
2 14½-oz. cans black beans, drained
1 c. beef bouillon or broth
1 tsp. oregano (may want more)
1 tsp. cumin (may want more)
2 cloves garlic, minced
Chopped green onions for topping, (optional)

In a large pot, sauté onions and peppers in olive oil until softened. Add remaining ingredients except green onions. Simmer at least 30 minutes. Serve in soup bowls over scoops of cooked rice. May top with green onions. Makes a meal for 4.

Poppy Seed Noodles

3 c. (dry measure) medium-wide noodles
2 to 4 Tbsps. butter
1 Tbsp. poppy seeds
Salt and pepper to taste

Cook and drain noodles. Add remaining ingredients. Serves 4.

Oh-So-Good Noodles

1½ c. (dry measure) medium or thin noodles
2 Tbsps. butter
4 green onions, coarsely chopped
1 clove garlic, minced
Salt and pepper to taste
2 Tbsps. fresh chopped parsley, (optional)

Cook noodles, drain, return to pot. Add remaining ingredients, stir to heat. Serves 2.

Linguini alla Roma

Linguini for 4 (8 ozs. average)
3 Tbsps. each: olive oil, butter
2 cloves garlic, finely minced
¼ c. fresh chopped parsley
Salt and pepper, freshly-ground preferred

Heat oil and butter, add garlic and parsley, salt and pepper. Pour hot over drained, hot linguini.

Noodles Alfredo

1½ Tbsps. butter
1 medium onion, finely chopped
2 c. chopped cooked ham or chicken
1 c. cream
12-oz. pkg. medium-sized noodles, cooked *al dente*
Freshly-grated Parmesan

Heat butter in a large skillet. Cook onion in butter slowly, until transparent. Add ham or chicken. Stir a few minutes. Add to hot cooked noodles along with more butter and a generous amount of Parmesan. Toss and serve immediately. Serves 4 to 6. *From Alfredo's in Rome via Virginia Bentley.*

Soups, Salads, Sandwiches & Sauces

Salads

*W*hen salad greens are unavailable or excessively expensive, look into the storage bin for pasta, beans, tuna, corn, artichoke hearts or something else to make an interesting salad.

Potato Salad

6 to 8 medium potatoes, cooked, peeled, diced
1 Tbsp. salad oil
3 Tbsps. vinegar
1 c. minced celery
¼ c. chopped green onions
2 hard-boiled eggs, chopped
4 slices bacon, cooked crisp, chopped
1 c. mayonnaise
Salt and pepper to taste
Paprika and/or chopped parsley (optional)

While potatoes are still warm, sprinkle with oil and vinegar. Mix with celery, green onions, chopped eggs and bacon. Fold in mayonnaise, season with salt and pepper. Chill. Before serving, if necessary, add additional mayonnaise. Dust with paprika or top with chopped parsley if desired. Serves 6.

Guacamole

1 large ripe avocado, peeled, mashed
1 Tbsp. fresh lemon juice
1 Tbsp. grated onion or 2 green onions, chopped
1 clove garlic, minced
Salt to taste
Tabasco sauce, chili powder or jalapeno peppers, finely chopped, to taste

Mix ingredients. To retard browning, press avocado seed into center of mixture, sprinkle mixture with lemon juice, cover. Remove seed when serving. Serves 2 to 4.

Simple Spinach Salad

10-oz. bag fresh spinach, washed, dried, torn into bite-size pieces
1 small red onion, thinly sliced
1 medium tomato, diced

Arrange in large salad bowl, or individual bowls, toss with the following dressing.

2 Tbsps. red wine vinegar
1 tsp. sugar
1 Tbsp. catsup
Pinch of pepper
½ c. salad oil
1 clove garlic, minced

OPTIONAL ADDITIONS: sliced fresh mushrooms, sliced water chestnuts, crisp, crumbled bacon, chopped hard-boiled egg, croutons. Serves 4.

Corn Salad

11-oz. can white shoe peg corn
¼ c. chopped cucumber
2 Tbsps. chopped scallions
¼ c. Kraft Zesty Italian Dressing or similar

Drain and rinse corn. Marinate corn, cucumber and scallions in dressing in covered container several hours. Serve as is or spoon over shredded lettuce and top with diced tomatoes. May pass extra dressing. About 2 c., 3 to 4 servings. Optional additions: sliced radishes, diced peppers, minced celery, slivered carrots. *Shirley Mayhew.*

Crunchy Salad with Green Peas

Drain a can of good quality small early peas. Add to taste chopped green onions, cucumber and celery. Make a dressing of mayonnaise (or half mayonnaise and half plain yogurt) mixed with salt, pepper and a bit of curry powder. Refrigerate until cold.

Black Bean Salad

A light salad with lime juice for the dressing, Jane Catlin's side dish salad is prepared quickly by mixing any of the ingredients desired. Chill before serving. Good with Mexican meals.

16-oz. can small black beans, rinsed, drained
Finely diced red onion, carrots, celery
Chopped green onions or dried chives
Chopped parsley or sprinkling of dried parsley
Fresh lime juice

Tabbouleh

1 c. bulgur wheat (cracked wheat)
¾ c. chopped parsley
¼ c. finely chopped mint
½ c. finely chopped scallions
¼ c. diced cucumber
2 medium tomatoes, diced
2 or more tablespoons olive oil
4 or more tablespoons fresh lemon juice
Salt and freshly ground pepper to taste

Place cracked wheat in a bowl, add boiling water just to cover. Cover bowl, let stand an hour or more to absorb water, drain, squeeze as dry as possible. Fluff with a fork. Add remaining ingredients, refrigerate, covered. Arrange on sliced romaine or scoop up with a leaf of romaine. Keeps well a few days in refrigerator. Approximately 4 to 6 servings.

Three Bean Salad

8-oz. can cut wax beans, drained
8-oz can cut green beans, drained
1 c. drained red kidney beans
1 small onion, finely chopped
¼ c. vinegar
¼ c. salad oil
2 Tbsps. sugar
½ tsp. salt
¼ tsp. pepper

Mix beans and onion. Combine remaining ingredients, pour dressing over beans, cover, chill. About 3 cups. Keeps well refrigerated.

Seashell Macaroni Salad with Dill

12-ozs. tiny shell macaroni, cooked, drained
1½ c. chopped scallions
1½ c. thinly sliced radishes
1 c. finely chopped green pepper
8-oz. can corn, rinsed, drained, or,
1 c. cooked fresh or frozen corn
1 c. mayonnaise
⅓ c. sour cream
1 Tbsp. Dijon mustard
1 clove garlic, minced
1 tsp. dill weed

Mix macaroni, scallions, radishes, peppers and corn in a salad bowl. Combine remaining ingredients for dressing, mix with salad, cover and chill. Serves 6 to 8. A favorite summer supper with sliced ham and sliced tomatoes.

Macaroni Salad with Ham

8 ozs. elbow macaroni
2 Tbsps. Italian dressing
¾ c. mayonnaise
1 tsp. Dijon mustard
1 c. diced cooked ham (deli-ham will do)
1 c. thinly sliced radishes
½ c. chopped green onions
Salt and pepper to taste

Cook macaroni, drain. While still warm, moisten with Italian dressing. Mix mayonnaise and mustard. Add to macaroni. Add remaining ingredients, cover and chill. Serves 4. Before serving, add additional mayonnaise or Italian dressing if needed to moisten.

Pasta Salad with Artichoke Hearts

Chop the artichokes from a 6½-oz. jar of marinated artichokes. Add the artichokes, and the marinade, to 8 ozs. cooked pasta twists or other pasta. Add other ingredients you may like, such as diced peppers, pimento, ham, corn, peas, cubes of cheese. Smooth out salad with a little mayonnaise. Serves 6 or more.

Greek Salad

For 4, layer in a large salad bowl, or in individual bowls, all or some of the following:

Shredded or torn romaine or mixed lettuces
1 cucumber, thinly sliced
1 medium red onion, thin rings
1 medium green pepper, thin rings
2 ripe tomatoes, cut into wedges, or
Cherry tomatoes, halved if large
8 radishes, thinly sliced
16 large black pitted olives, halved

Just before serving mix with this dressing:

2 Tbsps. fresh lemon juice
½ c. olive oil
1 clove garlic, minced
¼ tsp. salt
¼ freshly ground pepper
Pinch oregano

Use 1 c. crumbled feta cheese to top salad(s).

Overnight Salad

½ medium head iceberg lettuce, shredded
½ c. each: celery, red or green pepper, diced
1 pkg. frozen tiny peas, thawed, uncooked, dried
2 hard-boiled eggs, sliced
½ c. chopped red onion
1 c. mayonnaise
¼ c. salad oil
2 Tbsps. sugar
¼ c. grated Parmesan
1 c. grated cheddar
8 slices bacon, fried crisp, crumbled

In shallow serving dish, such as 9x13 Pyrex, layer lettuce, celery, peppers, peas, eggs and onion. Mix mayonnaise, oil, sugar and Parmesan. Smooth over salad. Distribute cheese and bacon over top. Cover tightly. Refrigerate at least 8 hours. Spoon from dish or toss lightly to serve 8 to 10.

Twenty-Four Hour Cabbage Slaw

1 large head cabbage, cored, chopped fine
½ green pepper, chopped
1 small onion, chopped
1 carrot, grated
½ c. oil
½ c. sugar
½ c. cider vinegar
1 tsp. celery salt

Combine cabbage, onion, pepper, carrot. Mix oil, sugar, vinegar and celery salt in a saucepan. Bring to a full boil. Remove from heat and pour over the vegetables. Toss gently. Cover tightly. Refrigerate 24 hours before serving. Serves 8 to 12. *Joan Klug.*

Chicken and Wild Rice Salad

6 oz. box Long Grain and Wild Rice, cooked
3 c. cooked and cubed chicken
2 stalks celery, finely chopped
1 Granny Smith (or other tart) apple, peeled, cubed
1 c. seedless green or red grapes, halved
2 Tbsps. minced fresh parsley
½ c. chopped walnuts or pecans (optional)
½ c. mayonnaise
4 Tbsps. cider vinegar
2 Tbsps. lemon juice
1 Tbsp. grainy mustard
½ tsp. sugar
¼ tsp. tarragon or thyme (or 1 tsp. of one, fresh)

Mix salad ingredients. Whisk together dressing ingredients. Pour dressing over salad. Refrigerate at least 2 hours before serving. Serves 8.

Notes / Extra Recipe

Basic Shrimp Salad

Mix 1 lb. cooked shrimp, diced, with 1 Tbsp. fresh lemon juice, ¼ c. minced celery, ¼ c. mayonnaise, salt and pepper to taste. Chill. Add more mayonnaise if needed. Serves 2.

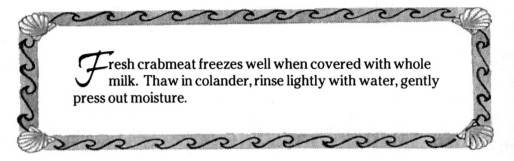

*F*resh crabmeat freezes well when covered with whole milk. Thaw in colander, rinse lightly with water, gently press out moisture.

Avocado and Crabmeat Salad

   1 lb. fresh crabmeat, lump preferred, all shell removed
   2 Tbsps. red wine vinegar
   1 tsp. Dijon mustard
   1 clove garlic, minced
   ½ tsp. salt, pinch of pepper
   ½ c. salad oil
   3 Tbsps. fresh lemon juice
   Mayonnaise
   2 large ripe avocados, halved

A few hours before serving, place crabmeat in non-aluminum mixing bowl. Make an oil and vinegar dressing of the vinegar, mustard, garlic, salt, pepper and oil. Drizzle a little of this dressing over crabmeat and sprinkle on the lemon juice. Mix gently, cover to marinate. Just before serving, mix in a little more dressing and enough mayonnaise to bind lightly. Place avocado halves on soft lettuce leaves on serving plates, fill with crabmeat. Serves 4.

Crabmeat Salad

Carefully remove any shell from crabmeat. Mix 1 lb. lump crabmeat with ½ c. finely chopped celery. Add to crabmeat. Mix ¼ c. mayonnaise, 2 Tbsps. lemon juice, a dash of paprika and some salt and pepper for dressing. Gently mix with the crab and celery, adding more mayonnaise if needed to moisten. Serves 3 to 4.

Marinated Tomatoes

4 to 6 large tomatoes, thickly sliced
1 large red or white onion, thinly sliced
⅓ c. salad oil
⅓ c. olive oil
⅓ c. red wine vinegar
½ tsp. salt
⅛ tsp. pepper
½ tsp. dried basil
½ tsp. oregano
1 clove garlic (remove before serving)
½ c. fresh chopped parsley (optional)

Alternate tomato and onion slices in serving bowl or plastic container. Make dressing of remaining ingredients except parsley. Pour over tomatoes and onions, marinate chilled several hours until serving. Drain off most of the dressing, sprinkle with parsley if available. Serves 6 to 8. Marinade may be used to dress a green salad.

Tomatoes with Mozarella

Alternate tomato slices with thin slices of mozzarella cheese. Sprinkle with chopped fresh basil (stems removed). Chill, covered. At serving time, drizzle lightly with oil and vinegar dressing.

Marinated Green Beans with Onions

2 lbs. young green beans
2 medium onions, thinly sliced
4 Tbsps. white vinegar
1 Tbsp. fresh lemon juice
½ c. olive oil
1 tsp. salt
¾ tsp. sugar
½ tsp ground pepper
2 Tbsps. finely chopped fresh parsley (optional)

Marinate beans and onions in dressing several hours. Drain and serve scattered with parsley. Serves 6 to 8.

My Chicken Salad

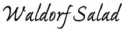

2 c. diced cooked chicken
½ to ¾ c. finely chopped celery
2 Tbsps. finely chopped green onion
1 Tbsp. fresh lemon juice
1 c. mayonnaise
Salt and pepper

Mix chicken, celery and green onion. Sprinkle with lemon juice. Refrigerate, covered. Shortly before serving, add mayonnaise, season with salt and pepper. Refrigerate, covered, if not serving immediately. Serves 2 to 3..

Waldorf Salad

Firm red apples, washed, unpeeled, diced to make 2 c.
1 c. diced celery
⅓ c. coarsely chopped walnuts
½ c. mayonnaise

Mix, serve as is or on lettuce leaves.

Cole Slaw

2½ c. shredded cabbage
1 c. finely shredded carrots
½ c. mayonnaise
½ c. sour cream
1 Tbsp. vinegar
1 to 2 tsps. seasoned salt
Minced parsley

Mix all but parsley. Sprinkle on parsley.

Cottage Cheese with Fruit

Mix cottage cheese with a little mayonnaise to moisten. Surround with mandarin orange segments, sliced kiwi fruit and/or chunks of fresh or canned pineapple. *Jane Catlin.*

Oil and Vinegar Dressings

Best whisked in a small bowl. First pour in the vinegar or lemon juice, then whisk in the oil gradually until the dressing is creamy. Whisk in the seasonings. A pepper mill is needed for freshly-ground pepper.

Basic French Dressing

¼ c. red wine vinegar
¾ c. olive oil, salad oil or a mixture
1 tsp. salt, ¼ tsp. pepper

Whisk or shake vigorously. For variety, add garlic or chopped fresh herbs, such as, basil, oregano, tarragon.

Dijon French Dressing

2 Tbsps. red wine vinegar
½ c. olive oil
¼ c. salad oil (I like Wesson)
1 Tbsp. Dijon mustard (I like Grey Poupon)
Salt (scant) and pepper to taste
2 Tbsps. chopped parsley or 2 tsps. dried

Blue Cheese Dressing

2 Tbsps. red wine vinegar
6 Tbsps. vegetable oil,
   olive oil or a mixture
1 Tbsp. dry mustard
1 clove garlic, minced
½ c. crumbled blue cheese

Pour vinegar into medium bowl. Whisk in oil a little at a time until mixture is creamy. Whisk in dry mustard and garlic. Stir in cheese. Serve over tossed greens. *P. Franey.*

French Dressing with Garlic

2 Tbsps. red wine vinegar
½ c. olive oil
1 tsp. Dijon mustard
½ tsp. paprika
¼ tsp. salt, pepper to taste
1 clove garlic, minced

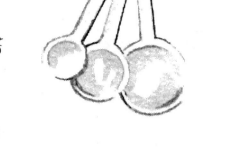

My Favorite French Dressing

¼ c. red wine vinegar
¼ c. olive oil
½ c. salad oil
½ tsp. each: salt, sugar
¼ tsp. each: paprika, dry mustard
Pinch each: pepper, thyme
¼ tsp. Worcestershire sauce

Put vinegar into small bowl. Whisk in oil a little at a time until thickened. Whisk in seasonings. Or, shake everything in a salad dressing bottle. About 1 cup.

Italian Dressing

⅓ c. each red wine vinegar, olive oil, salad oil
½ tsp. each: salt, sugar, dried parsley
¼ tsp. each: oregano, basil
⅛ tsp. pepper
1 clove garlic, minced or left whole (optional)

Whisk oils into vinegar until creamy. Whisk in seasonings. May put garlic clove on a toothpick, remove after a day or so. About 1 cup.

Catalina Dressing

1 can Campbell's condensed tomato soup, undiluted
¾ c. cider (or white) vinegar
½ c. salad oil
¼ c. sugar
1 Tbsp. Worcestershire sauce
1 tsp. each: salt, dry mustard, paprika
¼ tsp. onion powder

Whisk ingredients until well blended. Store in refrigerator. About 2 cups.

Creamy Blue Cheese Dressing

1 c. sour cream
¾ c. mayonnaise
Dash each: garlic powder, white pepper
4 ozs. blue cheese, crumbled

Do not add salt. Refrigerate.

Easy Cole Slaw Dressing

½ c. sour cream
½ c. mayonnaise
Lemon juice to taste
Salt and pepper to taste

Thousand Island Dressing

1 c. mayonnaise
3 Tbsps. chili sauce
1 Tbsp. chopped green pepper
1 tsp. each: chives, pimento, chopped

Mix to make about 1¼ cups.

QUICK VERSION: Mix 1 c. mayonnaise with ¼ to ½ c. chili sauce and 1 Tbsp. sweet relish.

Poppy Seed or Celery Dressing

¼ c. white vinegar
½ c. salad oil
½ c. sugar
½ tsp. dry mustard
⅛ tsp. salt
1 Tbsp. minced onion
¾ Tbsp. poppy seeds or celery seeds

Pour vinegar into a medium bowl. Whisk in oil until creamy. Whisk in sugar, dry mustard and salt. Add onion and poppy seeds. About 1 c. for fruit salads. Store in refrigerator.

Soups

Spinach Soup with Chopped Clams

10-oz. pkg. frozen chopped spinach
1 or 2 6½-oz. cans chopped clams
2 Tbsps. butter
1 medium onion, finely chopped
4 Tbsps. flour
2 c. chicken broth or 2 14½-oz. cans
¼ c. clam juice
¾ c. spinach liquid
Pinch ground nutmeg
Tarragon, salt and pepper to taste
½ c. cream or milk
Parmesan (optional)

Thaw spinach, reserving liquid. Drain clams, reserving clam juice. Melt butter in a large pot. Saute onions until softened. Over low heat, stir in flour slowly. Stir constantly 2 minutes. Gradually add stock, stirring constantly until thickened. Boil briefly, reduce heat, add spinach, clams, seasonings, clam juice and spinach juice. Simmer until hot, stir in cream or milk, adding more if needed to thin. Pass Parmesan if desired. About 1 qt. Serves 4. *Jo Gabeler Brooks.*

Spinach and Tortellini Soup

Add slivers of fresh spinach to boiling beef broth. Cook a few minutes, reduce heat, add cooked tortellini (the cheese-filled tortellini is good) and a pinch of red pepper flakes. Heat through and serve with Parmesan.

Vegetable Soup

3 Tbsps. olive oil
1 large onion, coarsely chopped
3 ribs celery, coarsely chopped
2 cloves garlic, minced
2 14½-oz. cans beef broth
3 beef bouillon cubes
3 c. water
14½-oz. can tomatoes, with juices, chopped
¼ tsp. oregano
¼ tsp. basil
Salt and pepper to taste
Vegetables of choice and Parmesan

Heat oil in a large pot. Sauté onion, celery and garlic until softened. Add broth, bouillon cubes, water, tomatoes and seasonings. Bring to a boil. Reduce heat. Add slivered or chopped fresh vegetables desired, such as, carrots, cabbage, corn, zucchini, spinach, beans, parsley. Cook over low heat, partially covered, about 45 minutes. (If using frozen or canned vegetables, add near the end of the cooking time.) Serve with Parmesan. About 2 quarts.

Corn Chowder

4 slices bacon
2 Tbsps. bacon fat
1 medium onion, chopped
3 medium potatoes, diced
14½-oz. can chicken broth
Salt and coarse-ground pepper to taste
11-oz. can corn niblets, rinsed
2 c. half-and-half or milk or a mixture

Cook bacon until crisp in a large pot. Set bacon aside, discard all but 2 Tbsps. fat. Add onions, cook over low heat until soft and golden, 5 to 10 minutes. Add potatoes and broth, salt and pepper, cook until potatoes are tender, 20 to 30 minutes. Add corn and cream or milk, heat through. Top each serving with crumbled bacon. About 1½ qts. for 4 bowls or 6 cups.

Mushroom Soup

The ideal way to use up leftover mushrooms.

1 Tbsp. butter
1 to 2 c. finely chopped fresh mushrooms
4 green onions, finely chopped
2 cloves garlic, minced
14½-oz. can beef broth
½ tsp. Worcestershire sauce
Salt and pepper to taste

In a medium saucepan, sauté mushrooms, green onions and garlic in butter until soft. Add broth and seasonings. Heat through. Serves 2.

Egg Drop Soup

3 c. chicken broth
2 tsps. cornstarch
1 Tbsp. water
1 egg, fork-beaten
Chopped green onions

Bring broth to a boil. Mix cornstarch and water, add to boiling broth. Stir until soup is slightly thickened. Remove soup from heat, drizzle in whipped egg. Top with chopped green onion. For 2 bowls or 3 cups. For 4 cups, add only 1 additional cup of broth.

Tuscan Bean Soup

Italian or French bread
2 Tbsps. olive oil
2 14½-oz. cans chicken broth or 4 c. homemade
Thinly-sliced onion rings
15-oz. can Great Northern white beans, drained
Garlic salt
Parmesan

In a small skillet, toast 4 slices bread in olive oil. Place in bottoms of soup bowls. Place about 3 onion rings on each piece of bread. Heat broth, add drained beans, season with garlic salt, spoon over bread. Pass Parmesan. Serves 4. To serve 6, add an extra can of broth. Serve the soup with the rest of the bread.

Chicken Broth with Rice

6 c. chicken broth or 3 14½-oz. cans
⅓ c. uncooked rice
¼ c. fresh chopped parsley
2 green onions, chopped
Salt and pepper to taste

Bring broth to a boil, add remaining ingredients. Cover, cook at a low boil until rice is tender, about 20 minutes. Serves 4.

Lentil Soup

1 Tbsp. olive oil
1 c. each, coarsely
   chopped: onion, celery
1 c. peeled diced potatoes
½ c. finely chopped carrots
1 clove garlic, chopped
½ c. dry lentils, rinsed
6 c. water
4 beef bouillon cubes
28-oz. can tomatoes chopped
   with juices
2 tsps. dried parsley or
   2 Tbsps. fresh, chopped
¼ tsp. oregano or basil
Salt and pepper to taste
About 1 Tbsp. bottled Maggi
   Seasoning (optional)
Smoked sausage, such as, kielbasa (optional)

Heat oil in a large pot. Sauté vegetables until softened. Add remaining ingredients, and sliced smoked sausage. Bring to a boil. Reduce heat, simmer, partially covered, about 45 minutes. Makes about 2 qts.

American Style Minestrone

2 Tbsps. olive oil
1 lb. lean ground beef
1 large onion, chopped
2 cloves garlic, minced
3 14½-oz. cans tomatoes, with juice, chopped
6 c. water, 6 beef bouillon cubes
1 c. sliced celery
½ tsp. each: salt, basil, oregano
¼ tsp. each: thyme, pepper
1 c. thinly sliced cabbage
½ c. broken-up uncooked spaghetti
8-oz. can each: corn, green beans, peas or other vegetables desired
Parmesan

Heat oil in large pot. Brown beef with onion and garlic, drain off fat. Add tomatoes, water, bouillon cubes, celery and seasonings. Bring to a boil. Add cabbage and pasta, simmer until cooked. Add vegetables, heat through. Pass the Parmesan. About 1½ qts., serves 6.

French Onion Soup

Since our boating "china" is not oven-proof, I put a thick slice of French bread in the bottom of the bowls, ladle in the boiling soup, which melts the cheese sprinkled on top.

4 Tbsps. butter
4 large onions, very thinly sliced
1 Tbsp. flour
1 tsp. each: Dijon mustard, Worcestershire
2 14½-oz. cans beef broth
4 beef bouillon cubes, 4 c. water
Salt and freshly ground pepper to taste
Grated Swiss and grated Parmesan
French bread

Melt butter in large pot. Sauté onions about 30 minutes until soft and golden. Sprinkle flour over onions, stir until smooth. Mix in mustard and Worcestershire. Add broth, bouillon cubes and water. Bring to a boil. Simmer until ready to serve. Spoon hot soup over bread, sprinkle each serving with about 2 Tbsps. grated Swiss cheese and a dusting of Parmesan. About 2 qts. for 6 large bowls. Serve extra bread.

Stracciatella

14½-oz. can chicken broth or 2 c, homemade
1 c. slivered fresh spinach
Pinch nutmeg (optional)
Freshly-ground black pepper
1 egg, fork-whipped
Parmesan
Croutons (optional)

Bring the broth to a boil, add spinach, nutmeg, if desired, and pepper. Cook a few minutes, reduce to a simmer. Stirring in one direction, add egg in a slow steady stream. Immediately remove from heat, pour in bowls. Serves 2. Top with Parmesan and, if you wish, croutons.

Shrimp Bisque

¾ lb. shrimp, cooked, deveined
2 Tbsp. each: butter, flour
3 c. half-and-half
Salt, pepper, Worcestershire, dry sherry, to taste
Additional cream if desired
Paprika

Melt butter in medium pot over medium heat. Stirring, cook butter and flour a few minutes. Add cream gradually, stirring until thickened. Season, add shrimp, thin with more cream if necessary. Sprinkle lightly with paprika. Serves 4.

Galley Clam Chowder

2 slices bacon, diced
¼ c. finely chopped onion
6½-oz. can chopped clams, with liquor
10½-oz. can cream of potato soup
1 soup can milk
Freshly-ground black pepper to taste
Butter (optional)

In a medium saucepan, stirring frequently, sauté bacon with onion until bacon is lightly browned. Drain off fat. Add remaining ingredients except butter. If desired, add a dab of butter to each piping hot serving. For 2 bowls or 3 cups.

Oyster Stew

1 pint fresh oysters, drained
2 Tbsps. butter
1 quart half-and-half
Salt and freshly-ground black pepper
Dash of Worcestershire sauce

Sauté oysters in butter until they curl around the edges. Add remaining ingredients, heat through. Serves 4.

Manhattan Clam Chowder

2 14½-oz. cans stewed tomatoes
2 6-oz. cans chopped clams, drained, reserve clam juice
½ c. bottled clam juice
3 small potatoes (red are nice), diced
1 clove garlic, minced
⅛ tsp. red pepper flakes
Salt and pepper to taste
1 small zucchini, diced
3 Tbsps. pesto sauce (optional)

Puree tomatoes or chop finely with their juices. Pour into a large saucepan. Add broth drained from clams to pan. Add bottled clam juice. Add potatoes, garlic, pepper flakes, salt and pepper. Bring to a boil, reduce heat, simmer uncovered 15 minutes, stirring occasionally. Add zucchini, simmer 5 minutes. Add clams, and, if desired, the pesto sauce. Stir to blend. Serves 4. *Claire Harris*.

Crabmeat Bisque

An unusual combination of soups results in a creamy pink and delicate bisque.

10½-oz. can condensed green pea soup
10½-oz. can condensed tomato soup
¾ c. chicken broth or bouillon
3 c. half-and-half
½ lb. crabmeat, all shell removed
1 jigger sherry

Combine soups and broth or bouillon. Bring to a boil. Reduce heat. When simmering, add half-and-half, crabmeat and sherry. Stir gently, cook only until warm throughout. Serves 4. *Jr. League, Memphis*.

Cream of Chicken Soup

3 Tbsps. each: butter, flour
2 c. chicken broth
1 c. milk or half-and-half
1 Tbsp. dried parsley
1 tsp. dried chives
Salt to taste

Melt butter in medium saucepan over moderate heat. Gradually add flour, stir constantly to cook a few minutes. Slowly add liquids, stir constantly until thickened. Add seasonings, and, stirring constantly, simmer at least 10 minutes to blend flavors. For 3 cups.

Cream of Spinach Soup

6 Tbsps. each: butter, flour
2 c. chicken broth
4 c. milk
2 tsps. dried chives
Salt, cayenne and pepper to taste
Dash nutmeg, (optional)
1 box frozen chopped spinach, thawed and drained

Heat butter in large saucepan. Add flour, stirring constantly, cook a few minutes. Stirring, gradually add liquids, then seasonings. Cook until smooth and thickened. Add well-drained spinach, and, stirring, heat through. 4 generous servings.

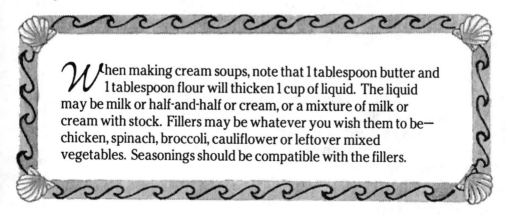

When making cream soups, note that 1 tablespoon butter and 1 tablespoon flour will thicken 1 cup of liquid. The liquid may be milk or half-and-half or cream, or a mixture of milk or cream with stock. Fillers may be whatever you wish them to be—chicken, spinach, broccoli, cauliflower or leftover mixed vegetables. Seasonings should be compatible with the fillers.

Spanish Gazpacho

3 6-oz. cans tomato juice or 18 ozs.
1 c. beef bouillon
2 Tbsps. each: olive oil, red wine vinegar
1 Tbsp. lemon juice
2 large ripe tomatoes, peeled, diced
½ c. chopped green pepper
½ c. peeled and seeded cucumber, chopped
¼ c. chopped green onion
1 clove garlic, minced
Dash each: Tabasco, Worcestershire
Salt and freshly-ground black pepper
Croutons

Mix ingredients in large non-aluminum bowl or pitcher. Chill. Serve with plain croutons. 4 large bowls or 6 cups.

Vichyssoise (Cold Potato Soup)

A galley staple, instant potato buds, thickens this tasty soup.

14½-oz. can chicken broth or 2 c. homemade
½ c. instant potato buds (I use Betty Crocker)
1 tsp. dried chives or 1 Tbsp. fresh, chopped
Salt and pepper
About ¼ c. milk or cream to thin

Bring broth to a boil. Stir in potato buds, reduce heat, stir to blend. Add chives, salt and pepper. Simmer gently 5 to 10 minutes. Add cream or milk to thin. Chill thoroughly Serves 2.

Chilly Chicken with Dill

10½-oz. can cream of chicken soup
1 soup can milk
½ c. finely chopped cucumber
About ½ tsp. dried chives
About ½ tsp. dill weed

Mix soup and milk. Chill. Top each serving with cucumbers and a sprinkling of chives and dill.

Breads

*F*or simplicity on the boat, we usually use mixes for muffins and loaves of specialty breads. We also use refrigerated tubes of breads and biscuits. Bisquick is a great staple for biscuits, coffee cake, and pancakes.

Puffies

Buy vacuum-packed, refrigerated baking powder or buttermilk biscuits sold in a tube. Separate biscuits, cut into quarters. Heat sufficient oil (I use Wesson) in a large skillet to nearly cover biscuits. When oil is hot, but not smoking, add about 8 biscuit quarters. Continuously turn over and over with a slotted spoon, removing to paper towels to drain as they get puffy and golden brown. (This does not take long.) Add a few biscuit sections as a few are removed. Sprinkle the Puffies with granulated sugar, or cinnamon sugar, and serve hot. A can of 6 biscuits makes 24 Puffies. Since people love these, better buy 2 cans of biscuits for more than 3 or 4.

French Toast

    4 slices bread
    1 egg, dash of salt
    1 c. milk
    ½ tsp. vanilla (optional)
    Dash cinnamon (optional)
    4 Tbsps. butter
    Maple syrup, powdered sugar, cinnamon sugar, sweetened fruit or
        other topping

Whip egg with a little salt in a shallow dish. Stir in milk, and, if desired, vanilla and cinnamon. Heat butter in a large skillet. Dip bread in milk mixture. Let excess run off. Turning occasionally, fry bread slices in the butter in the skillet until bread is firm and golden brown, about 10 minutes.

Cinnamon Toast

Toast bread, butter while hot. Sprinkle with a mixture of cinnamon sugar, 1 part cinnamon to 4 parts sugar. Mixture may be kept in a shaker.

French Bread Monterey

Very popular. Slice Italian or French bread into individual slices. Spread 6 to 8 slices with the following mixture to serve 4.

2 Tbsps. butter,
2 Tbsps. Parmesan
2 Tbsps. minced onion
¼ c. mayonnaise
⅛ tsp. Worcestershire sauce

Preheat oven to broil. Place bread slices on foil-lined baking sheet. Spread with butter mixture. Set baking sheet in middle of oven. Broil until browned and bubbly, 3 to 5 minutes. Watch carefully to prevent burning. *Jan Weese.*

Garlic Bread

1 medium-size loaf French or Italian bread
½ c. softened or melted butter
2 cloves garlic, finely minced
¼ c. finely chopped parsley (optional)

Slice bread vertically nearly to bottom crust. Mix butter and garlic, and, if desired, parsley. Spread soft butter or pour melted butter on each slice. Wrap in foil. Bake in preheated 350-degree oven 20 minutes. Open foil, bake 5 minutes longer. (May do less time at 375 or 400 degrees.) Serves 4 to 6.

Garlic and Herb Bread

Mix a pinch or two of 1 or 2 dried herbs with the butter, such as, basil, chervil, oregano, chives, marjoram, parsley.

Parmesan Bread

Split day-old rolls or sliced French or Italian bread with softened butter. Sprinkle lightly with seasoned salt and grated Parmesan cheese. Broil briefly to brown.

Blueberry Loaf

1½ c. all-purpose flour
2 tsps. baking powder
½ tsp. salt
1 egg
½ c. sugar
½ c. milk
2 Tbsps. melted butter
1 c. fresh blueberries

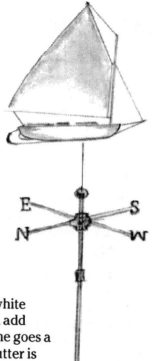

Sift dry ingredients together. Beat egg with a fork in a medium bowl. Cream sugar and egg. Add milk and butter. Fold in blueberries. Bake in loaf pan in preheated 350-degree oven 45 minutes or until done. (May take already sifted dry ingredients to boat in a baggie.)

Cayenne Toast

Remove crusts, if desired, from 2 slices firm white bread. In a skillet, heat about 2 tablespoons butter, add cayenne pepper to taste. Be careful, a little cayenne goes a long way. Turning frequently, sauté bread until butter is absorbed and bread is toasted. Cut into triangles. Serves 2.

Buttered Corn Biscuits

1 c. Bisquick
8-oz. can creamed corn
3 Tbsps. butter

Preheat oven to 400 degrees. Mix Bisquick and corn. Cut butter into bits, put into shallow baking pan with sides. Melt butter in the pan in the oven. Pour butter into a small cup. To make biscuits, put generous teaspoonfuls (about walnut-sized) of mix on baking sheet. They do not rise much so may be placed close together. Spoon butter over biscuits. Bake 12 to 15 minutes. For 15 to 18 biscuits. *D. DiSilvestro.*

Sandwiches

Hamburger Toast

4 slices firm-textured bread
Mustard, coarse-grained preferred
½ lb. lean ground beef, uncooked
Salt and pepper

Preheat broiler. Place bread slices on baking sheet. Toast lightly on one side in middle of oven. Spread untoasted sides to edges with mustard. With a fork, spread a thin layer of the uncooked ground beef to the very outside edges of the bread. Season with salt and pepper. Broil in mid-oven until done, 3 to 5 minutes. To vary, sprinkle with a little grated cheese a few minutes before done. Serves 2.

Sloppy Joes

1 onion, finely chopped
1 lb. ground round
1 tsp. minced garlic
8-oz. can tomato sauce
2 Tbsps. red wine vinegar
1 tsp. each: paprika, chili powder,
1 tsp. Worcestershire sauce
2 Tbsps. catsup

Sauté onion briefly in a small amount of oil. Add ground beef, cook until lightly browned. Add remaining ingredients, simmer about 15 minutes. Turn up heat, cook quickly until excess liquid is absorbed. Serve open-face or closed on split hamburger buns or split crusty rolls. Serves 4. Good with dill pickles and cole slaw.

English Muffins with Cheese and Ripe Olives

1 c. sliced ripe olives
1 c. shredded cheddar cheese
½ c. finely chopped green onion
½ c. mayonnaise
½ tsp. curry powder
Cayenne pepper to taste
3 English muffins, split

Preheat oven to 350 degrees. Combine cheese mixture. Spread generously on split muffins. Bake about 8 minutes until puffy and hot. Serves 3 to 6.

English Muffins with Onions and Parmesan

Split English muffins (Thomas brand preferred)
Onion disks
Mayonnaise
Parmesan

Slice onions about ⅛-inch thick without separating into rings. Preheat oven to broil. Place split muffins on a baking sheet (or foil pan), toast in mid-oven until lightly browned. Spread each muffin half lightly with mayonnaise. Cover completely with an onion disk. Spread rather lavishly with additional mayonnaise, then sprinkle generously with Parmesan. Place in lower part of oven. Broil at least 5 minutes to cook onion and brown cheese. *Julia Child, adapted.* Use Vidalia onions if available.

English Muffins with Bacon and Tomato

Preheat oven to broil. Broil 4 slices of bacon until half cooked. (A disposable foil pan is handy for this.) Toast 4 split muffins lightly. Drizzle with a little Italian dressing. Lay on thick slices of tomato, season with salt and pepper. Sprinkle with grated cheddar or other cheese. Dice bacon, distribute over cheese. Broil in mid-oven until bacon is cooked and cheese is melted. Serves 4.

Ham and Cheese Mini Morsels

Pepperidge Farm (or similar) small party rolls are nice for small sandwiches or the dinner rolls for larger sandwiches.

    1 pkg. party rolls or dinner rolls
    Thinly sliced baked or boiled ham
    Thinly sliced Monterey Jack or Swiss cheese
    Soft butter and coarse-grained or Dijon mustard

Slice the whole sheet of rolls through the middle to make one top layer and one bottom layer. Spread cut sides liberally with softened butter mixed with mustard to taste. Lay ham and cheese slices on bottom layer of rolls. Reassemble like a sandwich, return rolls to the foil container they came in. Cover completely with foil, heat in preheated 375-degree oven 8 minutes or until heated through. Cut into individual servings.

Beef Barbecue

    1½ lbs. boneless steak (round, sirloin)
    2 Tbsps. oil
    1 Tbsp. butter
    1½ c. catsup
    ⅓ c. water
    3 Tbsps. each: wine vinegar, lemon juice,
    Worcestershire sauce
    Tabasco sauce to taste
    1 large onion, finely chopped
    2 tsps. each: sugar, dry mustard
    1½ tsps. chili powder
    ¾ tsp. salt or to taste
    ¾ tsp. paprika or to taste

Slice steak into thin strips 2 to 3 inches long. Brown in oil and butter in skillet over moderately high heat. Cook in small batches, stirring constantly, set aside as done. Add remaining ingredients to skillet or a saucepan, bring to a boil. Reduce heat, return steak to pan, simmer about 15 minutes. Spoon into buns, open-face or closed. Serves 4 to 6.

Mini Pizzas

For 6 little pizzas, preheat oven to broil. Split 3 English muffins. Place on baking sheet in mid-oven to dry out cut surfaces slightly. Spread with pizza sauce, add favorite toppings including cheese. Broil in mid-oven until done.

Pizza Sauce

14½-oz. can tomatoes, drained, chopped
2 Tbsps. olive oil
1 small onion, halved
1 clove garlic, minced
1 bay leaf
1 beef bouillon cube
½ tsp. sugar
¾ tsp. oregano
Salt and pepper to taste

Mix ingredients in medium saucepan, simmer about 10 minutes. Remove onion and bay leaf. If necessary, boil to thicken. Good, too, for 1 large pizza.

Hot Pastrami Sandwiches

Spread bread or split rolls with Dijon mustard. Layer on thinly sliced pastrami and Swiss. Broil until cheese melts.

Grilled Ham and Cheese Sandwiches

Spread the outsides of rye bread lightly with butter. Fill sandwiches with thin slices of ham, thin slices of Jarlsberg or white cheddar cheese, and spread with coarse-grained mustard. Grill in a skillet until cheese melts and bread is browned on both sides.

Reuben Muffins

Preheat oven to broil. Split English muffins. Place on baking sheet to toast lightly. Cover muffin halves with thinly-sliced cooked corned beef, well-drained sauerkraut, a bit of Russian dressing, and sliced Swiss cheese. Place in lower part of oven, broil until cheese melts.

Terrific Tuna

Delightful for sandwiches or on rounds of wheat bread. Mixture may be used also to stuff garden-fresh tomatoes.

3½-oz. can albacore tuna, packed in spring water, drained
2 Tbsps. finely minced celery
1 Tbsp. finely minced onion
½ tsp. each: dill weed, curry powder
Salt and lemon juice to taste
Mayonnaise to moisten

Shred tuna completely with a fork. Mix with remaining ingredients. Chill. For 2 or 3 sandwiches, several canapés or 2 filled tomatoes. Sprinkle canapés and salads with a little extra dill weed.

Sliced Smoked Turkey

Good on whole wheat bread or in split pitas with slices of Monterey Jack, alfalfa sprouts and tomatoes. Spread bread or pitas with mayonnaise or brush with Italian dressing before filling.

Make Your Own Pitas

Cut favorite cheese slices into quarters. Tear lean ham slices into small pieces. Place in serving container, cover with Italian dressing, refrigerate covered. At serving time, split pita bread. Serve marinated ham and cheese and small bowls of shredded lettuce, chopped green onion, alfalfa sprouts and tiny tomato cubes.

Huge Hoagie

Split a loaf of French or Italian bread, brush cut sides with olive oil, some Italian dressing, and, if desired, spread on some mayonnaise. Add thin slices of onion, tomato, green pepper, Genoa salami and Provolone cheese. May make ahead. Refrigerate wrapped in plastic wrap. Cut into individual portions when serving.

The Long Loaf Sandwich

Split a loaf of French bread in half lengthwise. Spread cut sides lightly with Dijon mustard and mayonnaise. Layer with shredded lettuce, thin slices of cooked ham, thinly sliced cucumbers, slices of a good French brie and thin red pepper rings. Cut into 4 to 6 sandwiches. Delightful with chilled white wine.

Egg Salad

Chop 3 hard-boiled eggs. Mix about ¼ c. mayonnaise, 1½ tsps. Dijon mustard, ½ tsp. dried chives and ¼ tsp. dillweed. Mix with eggs, spread on wheat bread or pumpernickel.

Cream Cheese and Olive

Mix softened cream cheese with chopped pimento-stuffed olives, a little olive juice and a bit of mayonnaise.

Bacon, Lettuce, Tomato and Avocado Slices

This combination is wonderful on wheat bread or toast with mayonnaise to moisten.

Peanut Butter and Honey

Mix 4 Tbsps. peanut butter, 2 Tbsps. soft butter and 1½ Tbsps. honey for an energy-boosting sandwich.

Peanut Butter and Banana

Mix 1 ripe mashed banana with ¼ c. peanut butter and, if desired, 2 tsps. tart jelly.

Peanut Butter and Bacon

Spread 1 slice of bread with peanut butter, the other lightly with mayonnaise. Sprinkle crumbled bacon over 1 slice of bread and top with the other.

Smoked Salmon

Make sandwiches on dark bread with thinly sliced smoked salmon and thin slices of onion and tomato. Dress with mayonnaise.

Cream Cheese and Cucumber

Spread soft cream cheese and a little mayonnaise on wheat bread. Add a layer of tiny cubes of seeded cucumber and a layer of very finely minced onion. If desired, add thinly sliced tomato and alfalfa sprouts.

Sauces

My Tomato Sauce

My marinara sauce for spaghetti, cacciatore, parmigiana and more.
I freeze in pint containers.

¼ c. olive oil
1 medium onion, finely chopped
2 cloves garlic, minced
28-oz. can tomatoes, chopped
6-oz. can tomato paste
8-oz. can tomato sauce
14½-oz. can beef broth
3 Tbsps. fresh chopped parsley or 1 Tbsp. dried
1 tsp. each: sugar, salt, basil
2 tsps. oregano
Pepper to taste

Heat oil in a large saucepan. Add onion and garlic. Saute until softened.
Add remaining ingredients, bring to a boil. Reduce heat, and, stirring
occasionally, simmer partially covered at least 1 hour. About 6 cups.

Hap's Spaghetti Sauce Supreme

2 Tbsps. cooking oil
2 to 3 cloves garlic, diced
2 28-oz. cans Italian-style peeled or whole tomatoes-with-basil
12-oz. can Italian tomato paste, Contadina recommended
2 (or 1½) Tbsps. crushed oregano
2 (or 1½) Tbsps. crushed sweet basil
8 c. water
½ to 1 tsp. salt
6 to 12 links sweet (or hot) Italian sausage

Simmer covered 2½ to 3 hours. If too thin, remove cover until thickened.
Serves 6 to 8. Can be frozen in individual servings in zip-lock bags. *Hap Brooks.*
[**AUTHOR'S NOTE:** Delicious!]

Tomato Cream Sauce

4 Tbsps. each: butter, olive oil
¼ c. finely chopped onion
¼ c. finely chopped celery
¼ c. finely chopped carrots
28-oz. can Italian tomatoes, chopped
1½ tsps. salt or to taste
¼ tsp. sugar
½ c. heavy cream
Parmesan

Sauté onion, celery and carrots in oil and butter until slightly softened. Add tomatoes, salt and sugar. Stirring occasionally, simmer uncovered at least 45 minutes. Press through a strainer or colander, discard solids left behind. There will be about 2 c. of somewhat thin sauce. Reheat sauce, stir in cream. If desired, boil gently to reduce. Serve piping hot with hot pasta. Pass the Parmesan. 3½ to 4 c. Serves 3 to 4.

Sauce Verti (for beef-hot or cold)

¾ c. mayonnaise
¼ c. sour cream
1 Tbsp. each: dried chives, dried parsley
¾ tsp. dried tarragon
¾ tsp. dried dillweed

Cranberry Relish

1 each: lemon, orange
1½ c. fresh cranberries
2 c. dark brown sugar
1½ c. raisins
½ c. white vinegar
½ tsp. each: cinnamon, cloves, nutmeg
½ cinnamon stick

Quarter the fruits, remove seeds, dice. Put into a large pot with the cranberries. Add remaining, bring to a boil. Reduce heat, simmer 15 minutes. Remove cinnamon stick. Cool. Refrigerate. Serve with ham, turkey, chicken. A small jar of this is a nice gift for a friend. *Nadia Lasher.*

Picante Sauce

    1 c. finely chopped ripe tomato
    1½ Tbsps. seeded, chopped fresh jalapeno chilies
    2 Tbsps. finely chopped onion
    2 Tbsp. water
    1 Tbsp. lime juice
    ½ tsp. oregano

Combine and chill. About 1½ cups. Good with any Mexican meal.

Medium White Sauce

For creamed dishes, casseroles and vegetables.

    2½ Tbsps. butter
    3 Tbsps. flour
    2 c. milk
    ½ tsp. salt
    Pepper to taste

Melt butter in a medium saucepan over moderate heat. Gradually add flour, stirring to blend with butter. Cook and stir continuously without browning 2 to 3 minutes. Add milk gradually, stirring constantly. Bring to a boil, reduce heat, simmer at least 5 minutes. Stir occasionally. Add more milk for a thinner sauce. For 2 cups.

Sauce Mornay

Stir ¼ c. each grated Swiss and grated Parmesan into finished white sauce. Stir until cheese melts and sauce is smooth.

Thin White Sauce

For soups, use 1 Tbsp. each butter and flour and 1 c. milk. Make as above.

Lemon Butter

Add 1 Tbsp. fresh lemon juice to 4 Tbsps. melted butter. For vegetables, fish and shellfish. Good, too, with 1 Tbsp. fresh chopped parsley added.

Seafood Cocktail Sauce

½ c. each: chili sauce, catsup or all chili sauce
2 Tbsps. each: lemon juice, drained horseradish
¼ tsp. Tabasco
¼ tsp. Worcestershire
Mix and chill for about 1 c. sauce.

Tartar Sauce

1 c. mayonnaise
2 Tbsps. fresh minced parsley or 2 tsps. dried
2 tsps. minced onion
1 Tbsp. pimento-stuffed green olives, chopped
2 Tbsps. drained sweet relish

For about 1 c. for fish.

Easy Tartar Sauce

For each 2 Tbsps. mayonnaise, mix in 1 Tbsp. drained sweet relish. Add a little lemon juice if desired.

Blender Bearnaise

For special occasions with steak or beef fondue.

1 stick butter
3 egg yolks
2 Tbsps. fresh lemon juice
Scant ½ tsp. salt
Dash pepper
¼ tsp. dried tarragon
¼ tsp. parsley, crushed

Heat butter until hot and bubbly but not browned. Put remaining ingredients into blender container. Blend at low speed 5 seconds. Add hot butter very slowly, drop-by-drop, until mixture starts to thicken. Then add in a slow steady stream until thickened. For 4 for steaks, 6 for a fondue sauce. *Peg Wilson.*

NOTES: I use a measuring cup with a spout or a small pitcher to add droplets of butter. May make early, bring to room temperature.

Pesto Sauce

2 c. (packed) fresh basil leaves, stems removed, coarsely chopped
½ c. plus 1 Tbsp. good quality olive oil
3 Tbsps. finely chopped pine nuts (or walnuts)
1 Tbsp. coarsely chopped garlic
1 tsp. salt
½ tsp. freshly ground pepper
½ c. freshly grated Parmesan

(Do remove the bitter stems from the basil.) Put all ingredients, except Parmesan, in container of processor or blender. Blend until smooth. Add Parmesan, blend briefly or simply stir in the Parmesan. Serve with pasta, grilled fish, cold meat, omelets, French bread. To serve with pasta, toss pasta with a few tablespoons of soft butter. Thoroughly mix pesto sauce with the pasta. Try about one tablespoon pesto per serving of pasta. Store, refrigerated, about a week. Freezes well.

Mustard Sauce

Delicious on ham or roast beef sandwiches. Good with beef shish kebabs and beef fondue.

¼ c. mayonnaise
¼ c. sour cream or yogurt
1 Tbsp. dry mustard
1 tsp. dried chives
1 tsp. white vinegar

Blend well for about ½ cup.

Plum Sauce

1 c. plum jelly or chopped plum preserves
½ c. very finely chopped chutney,
Major Grey's preferred
1 Tbsp. each: white vinegar, sugar

Blend the ingredients until smooth. Serve with egg rolls, fried shrimp, pork or beef fondue. *Ginny Kiefer.*

Desserts

Desserts

*W*e serve simple desserts while cruising. often only fruit, or fruit along with sliced cheese. Cheddar, Edam, Camembert and Brie go well with many fruits, especially apples and pears. Plain crackers or sliced French bread are good with the cheese. Bowls of mixed fruits are refreshing, too, and often are enhanced by adding flavor-compatible liqueurs.

Certain cakes keep well on a boat. Fruit cake is one of these, and rum or whiskey-soaked cakes packed in tins. Pound cake lasts well, too, and may be made quite festive with a simple icing or served with a sauce.

Purchased and homemade cookies should be kept in covered containers. For entertaining, I often bring aboard bar cookies which I have made and frozen at home. On board, we sometimes make cookies from uncomplicated recipes.

By using refrigerated pie crusts or a box of pie crust mix, it is relatively easy to make pies. Take advantage of these and other prepared products to keep dessert-making easy. Elaborate desserts are made more easily at home.

Gourmet Grapes

Allow 1 lb. grapes for 4 to 6. For each serving, halve or quarter seedless green grapes. Arrange in individual dessert dishes. Spoon 2 tsps. cointreau or triple sec over each serving. Add a generous spoonful of sour cream. Sprinkle lightly with cinnamon, more generously with brown sugar, sifted if lumpy.

Spiked Watermelon

Mix about 6 c. watermelon balls or chunks with ⅓ c. each sugar and rum. Add 3 Tbsps. fresh lime juice.

Pineapple with Rum

Cut 1 fresh pineapple into bite-size pieces. Mix with 4 Tbsps. sugar and 2 Tbsps. dark rum, or to taste. Refrigerate several hours before serving to 4. *Sarah Gaede.*

Pineapple Dream

Mix well-drained canned pineapple chunks with 1 mini-marshmallow for each pineapple chunk. Generously cover with whipped cream. Stir gently to mix.

Dump Cake

Pour a 29-oz. can crushed pineapple, undrained, into buttered 9 x 13 pan. Pour on 3½-oz. can flaked coconut. Pour on yellow cake mix (dry). Cut up 2 sticks butter, dab over cake. Bake in preheated 350-degree oven 40 minutes or until brown. *Gloria Deming.*

Ambrosia

For each large seedless orange, peeled and cut into bite-size pieces, add 1 Tbsp. powdered sugar and 1 Tbsp. sweetened flaked coconut. Refrigerate.

New England Blueberry Slump

In a medium saucepan, mix a 15-oz. can blueberries packed in heavy syrup with 3 Tbsps. sugar, ½ tsp. ground cinnamon and ½ c. water. In a small bowl, mix 1⅛ c. Bisquick with ⅓ c. milk. Bring blueberry mixture to a boil. Drop about 8 small blobs of biscuit mix on top of berries. Cover closely, cook on low heat about 20 minutes. Serve dumplings with sauce spooned over them. Serves 4. Good with vanilla ice cream, too.

Tipsy Peaches

Peel and slice fresh peaches into a serving bowl. Add sugar to taste and a few generous splashes of rum. Cover with plastic wrap. Leave at room temperature about an hour to draw out juices from peaches. Good on pound cake, ice cream, yogurt or vanilla pudding.

Peaches and Cream

Simmer a 16-oz. can undrained sliced peaches with 1 Tbsp. butter and a cinnamon stick 5 minutes. Serve warm topped with a dollop of sour cream or whipped cream and a sprinkling of ground cinnamon. Serves 4.

Strawberries

Rinse, but do not hull, flavorful fresh strawberries. Blot dry. Pass serving bowls of sifted brown sugar and sour cream for dipping. Each person should have a small plate and take a spoonful of the sour cream, a spoonful of brown sugar and some berries. If preferred, stir enough brown sugar into 1 c. of sour cream to make it a rich caramel color. Refrigerate, provide cocktail picks for dipping berries.

Mixed Fruits with Coconut

3 large oranges, peeled, sliced
2 ripe bananas, sliced
1 small apple, cored, diced
¼ c. maraschino cherries, halved
Sugar to taste
¼ c. each: flaked coconut, chopped pecans

Mix fruits in a serving bowl, sweeten to taste with sugar. Chill thoroughly. Before serving, sprinkle with coconut and pecans. Serves 4.

Broiled Grapefruit

Cut grapefruit in half. Loosen sections, but leave in the grapefruit shell. Dot with tiny dabs of butter. Sprinkle with sugar and a little cinnamon. Broil about 4 inches from heat source about 8 minutes.

Banana Pudding

1 pkg. (¾ oz.) instant vanilla pudding
2 bananas
32 mini-marshmallows
Milk (optional)

Prepare pudding according to package directions. In each of 4 dessert dishes, layer some pudding, half a sliced banana, 8 mini-marshmallows and more pudding. When serving, top with milk if desired.

Apple Crisp

3 medium apples, Granny Smith preferred
2 Tbsps. sugar
⅛ tsp. each: nutmeg, cinnamon
Sprinkling of lemon juice
2 Tbsps. water
6 Tbsps. flour
Dash each: salt, cinnamon, nutmeg
4 Tbsps. butter

Place sliced, peeled apples in a small buttered baking dish. Mix sugar, nutmeg and cinnamon. Sprinkle over apples. Sprinkle with lemon juice and water. For topping, in medium bowl, mix flour, sugar, salt, cinnamon and nutmeg. Cut in butter or mix in with fingertips. Dab mixture over apples. Bake in 375-degree oven about 40 minutes. Serves 2 to 3.

Baked Bananas

2 firm ripe bananas, halved lengthwise
2 Tbsps. butter
¼ c. orange juice
2 Tbsps. honey or brown sugar
Cinnamon
2 Tbsps. rum

Preheat oven to 425 degrees. While preheating, melt butter in baking dish in oven. Lay bananas in baking dish, split side down. Spoon some butter over bananas. Pour orange juice over all, spoon on honey or brown sugar, dust lightly with cinnamon. Bake 5 to 10 minutes until bananas are warm but not soft. Add rum. Serve with sauce spooned over bananas. Serves 2. Delicious with vanilla yogurt, vanilla ice cream or pound cake.

Pears with Apricot Sauce

Heat 1 c. apricot preserves in a small saucepan. Stir in ⅓ c. dry vermouth. Spoon warm sauce over fresh pear halves, peeled, or over drained canned pear halves. Sauce for 4 servings.

Saratoga Torte

3 egg whites
1 c. sugar
1 tsp. each: vanilla, baking powder
14 Saltines, coarsely crumbled
¾ c. chopped walnuts or pecans
1 c. heavy cream
Unsweetened baking chocolate (optional)

Beat egg whites until almost stiff. Gradually add sugar. Combine crumbled crackers, nuts and baking powder. Fold into egg mixture. Add vanilla. Spread in 9-inch pie pan. Bake in preheated 350-degree oven 45 minutes. When cool, spread with slightly sweetened whipped cream. Refrigerate until cold. May grate unsweetened chocolate over the cream. Serves 6 to 8.

Strawberry Cake with Cream

Slice a prepared pound cake crosswise into thirds. Spread cut layers with strawberry preserves. Reassemble cake. Ice tops and sides with sweetened whipped cream. Garnish cake top with rows of fresh stemmed strawberries, tips pointing up. Refrigerate until serving time.

Layer Cake with Chocolate Icing

Slice a 12-oz. prepared pound cake crosswise into 3 or 4 layers. Melt a 6-oz. pkg. semi-sweet chocolate bits in a double boiler. Remove from heat, mix in ½ c. sour cream. Spread on cake layers, reassemble cake, ice the top. Store in refrigerator.

Rum Cake

Melt 4 Tbsps. butter over low heat, add ¼ c. water and ⅓ c. sugar. Boil gently about 5 minutes. Remove from heat, stir in ¼ c. rum. With an ice pick, puncture a pound cake half way through at about 1-inch intervals. Pour rum glaze slowly over cake. Let it soak in a while before eating. Store in refrigerator covered with plastic wrap.

Peach Sauce with Pineapple and Rum

Good over ice cream or frozen yogurt, pound cake, angel food cake and puddings.

½ c. peach or apricot preserves
½ c. canned crushed pineapple, drained
1 jigger rum or more to taste

Heat preserves in small saucepan to melt. Stir in pineapple and rum. Serve warm. B. Shreve.

Hot Fudge Sauce

2 squares unsweetened baking chocolate
1 c. sugar
5-oz. can evaporated milk
1½ tsps. butter
Pinch salt
1 tsp. vanilla

Heat all except vanilla in saucepan over medium heat. Stir frequently until chocolate melts. Stir in vanilla. Serve hot. About 1½ cups. Store in refrigerator. Thickens and smooths on standing. Reheat amount needed.

Marshmallow Fudge

5 oz. can evaporated milk
½ tsp. salt
1⅔ c. sugar
1½ c. chocolate chips
1½ c. mini marshmallows
1 tsp. vanilla
½ c. chopped pecans

Combine milk, salt and sugar in medium saucepan. Stirring, bring mixture to a boil, reduce heat, cook 5 minutes longer, stirring constantly. Remove from heat, add chocolate chips and marshmallows, stir until smooth. Add vanilla and pecans, spread in buttered 8-inch square pan. Cool before cutting into small squares. Store in refrigerator or freezer wrapped in plastic wrap.

Bread Pudding

1 egg
⅔ c. milk
1 Tbsp. melted butter
3 Tbsps. brown sugar
½ tsp. each: cinnamon, nutmeg
½ c. raisins
1 c. bread cubes (about 1½ slices)

Preheat oven to 350 degrees. Butter a small baking dish. Whisk egg in small bowl, beat in butter, milk, sugar and seasonings. Place bread cubes in bottom of baking dish, scatter raisins over bread, pour milk mixture over all. Bake about 35 minutes. Serve warm with cream or milk. Serves 2.

Apple Pie

6 large tart apples, peeled and sliced
½ c. granulated sugar
1 tsp. cinnamon, or cinnamon and nutmeg mixed
1 Tbsp. each: lemon juice, butter
2 crusts for 9-inch pie, Pillsbury's preferred

Preheat oven to 425 degrees. Line a pie plate with crust, fill heaping with apple slices. Mix sugar and cinnamon, sprinkle over apples. Sprinkle with lemon juice, dot with bits of butter. Cover with top crust, make slits in crust, bake about 45 minutes or until done.

Pecan Pie

3 eggs, slightly beaten
1 c. Karo light or dark corn syrup
¾ c. sugar
2 Tbsps. melted butter
1 tsp. vanilla
1½ c. chopped pecans
1 9-inch pie crust

Mix eggs, syrup, sugar, butter and vanilla. Stir in pecans. Pour into pie crust. Bake in 350-degree oven about 50 minutes. Serves 8.

Coconut Cookies with Kahlua

1⅓ c. loosely-packed sweetened coconut
⅓ c. sugar
2 Tbsps. each: flour, Kahlua
1 egg white

In a small bowl, gently mix the coconut, sugar, flour and Kahlua. Whisk egg white in medium bowl until frothy. Gently mix coconut mixture and egg white. Drop by rounded teaspoons on a greased cookie sheet. Bake in preheated 325-degree oven until firm. 20 little cookies take about 15 minutes to bake.

Date Cookies

½ c. softened butter (or margarine)
1 egg
2 tsps. vanilla
1 c. all-purpose flour
1 tsp. baking powder
½ tsp. salt
1 c. each: chopped pitted dates, shredded coconut, chopped walnuts

Beat butter or oleo, egg and vanilla with electric beater until smooth. In separate bowl, combine flour, baking powder and salt. Gradually add to creamed mixture. Beat until blended. Stir in dates, coconut and walnuts. Form dough into two ½-inch rolls, wrap in waxed paper, chill in freezer until firm enough to slice — 2 hours up to 1 month. Place slices on lightly greased cookie sheet and bake at 250 degrees about 10 minutes. About 5 dozen. Sugarless. Good for energy boost. *Mary Clapp.*

Hello Dolly Bar Cookies

- 1 stick butter
- 1 c. crushed Saltine crackers
- 1 c. coconut
- 1 c. chocolate chips
- 1 c. chopped pecans
- 1 14-oz. can sweetened condensed milk

Melt butter in 9x13 pan in preheated 350-degree oven. Layer remaining ingredients on order given. Bake 30 minutes. Cool before cutting.

Katherine Hepburn's Brownies

Easy to do on board or freeze at home to bring on board in the disposable pan.

- 1 stick butter
- 2 squares unsweetened chocolate
- 1 c. sugar
- 2 eggs
- ½ tsp. vanilla
- ¼ c. all-purpose flour
- ¼ tsp. salt
- 1 c. chopped walnuts (I use pecans)

Preheat oven to 325 degrees. Melt butter and chocolate together in a medium saucepan over low heat. Remove from heat, stir in sugar. Add eggs and vanilla. Beat the mixture well. Stir in flour and salt. Bake brownies in a buttered and floured 8-inch square pan about 40 minutes. Cool, cut into squares.

Date and Nut Squares

Q and E — that is, quick and easy. Make in one pan, bake in an 8-inch square foil pan, and freeze, or bake on board.

4 Tbsps. butter
1 c. dark brown sugar
2 eggs
½ c. flour
1 tsp. baking powder
¼ tsp. salt
½ c. chopped dates
¼ c. chopped pecans or walnuts
½ tsp. vanilla
Powdered sugar (optional)

Melt butter over low heat in a medium saucepan. Add brown sugar, stir briefly until melted and smooth. Remove from heat, cool. With a mixing spoon, beat in eggs one at a time. Stir in remaining ingredients. Bake in greased 8-inch square pan in preheated 350-degree oven, 25 to 30 minutes, until set. Cool. If desired, sprinkle with powdered sugar (a small sifter is handy for this), then cut into 16 squares.

Notes / Extra Recipes

Notes / Extra Recipes

Notes / Extra Recipes

Notes / Extra Recipes

Index

A

A la king, chicken · 55
Alfredo, noodles · 118
Alfredo, sauce, with
    chicken · 49
Alla Francese, chicken · 47
Alla Francese, veal · 101
Amandine, beans · 105
Amandine, scallops · 68
Ambrosia · 157
Appetizers · 23
Apple crisp · 158
Apple pie · 161
Apple rings, sautéed · 104
Apricot sauce,
    for pears · 159
Arroz con pollo · 56
Artichoke
    crab casserole · 64
    dip · 30
    potato salad · 123
    shrimp casserole · 76
    spread · 26
Asparagus
    with chicken · 49
    stir-fry · 104
Au gratin potatoes · 109

Avocado
    bacon, tomato · 149
    & crabmeat salad · 126
    dip · 27

B

Bacon & water
    chestnuts · 32
Baked
    bananas · 159
    beans · 106
    fish · 58, 59, 63
    oysters · 69
    rice · 116
Banana pudding · 158
Banana sunrise · 36
Basting sauce, for fish ·
    58, 84
Barbecue, beef · 146
Barbecue sauce,
    with chili powder · 78
    Mary Lou's · 79
    pineapple · 81
    Southern · 78
Bean, black, salad · 122
Bean, burger, casserole · 90

Bean, three, salad · 122
Beans
    baked · 106
    baked, with franks · 92
    green, amandine · 105
    green, fresh · 105
    green, marinated,
        salad · 127
    red, and rice · 108
Bean soup, Tuscan · 134
Bearnaise sauce · 153
Beef
    barbecue · 146
    Bolognese sauce · 88
    chipped, spread · 31
    dried, creamed · 86
    shish kebabs · 83
    stew · 86
    stroganov · 85
Beverages · 34
Biscuits, corn · 143
Bisque, crab · 138
Bisque, shrimp · 137
Black bean salad · 122
Black beans & rice · 117
Bloody Mary · 34
Blue cheese dressing · 129

Q-R

S

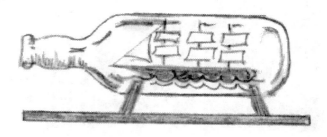